ACTION MOVIE
FREAK

by Action Flick Chick
KATRINA HILL

Published by

Krause Publications, a division of F+W Media, Inc.
700 East State Street • Iola, WI 54990-0001
715-445-2214 • 888-457-2873
www.krausebooks.com

To order books or other products call toll-free 1-800-258-0929
or visit us online at www.krausebooks.com

Front cover movie stills and posters: main photo: *Rambo III*-Carolco/The Kobal Collection; bottom photos, from left: *Aliens*-20th Century Fox/Heritage Auctions, *Die Hard*-20th Century Fox/Heritage Auctions, *Enter the Dragon*-Warner Bros./Heritage Auctions, *Commando*-20th Century Fox/Heritage Auctions, *Black Dynamite*-Ars Nova/The Kobal Collection, *Lara Croft: Tomb Raider*-Paramount/Heritage Auctions. **Back cover**: *Dirty Harry*-Warner Bros./The Kobal Collection. **Contents page**: *Rumble in the Bronx*-Golden Harvest/Heritage Auctions, *Magnum Force*-Warner Bros./Heritage Auctions.

ISBN-13: 978-1-4402-3208-4
ISBN-10: 1-4402-3208-3

Front cover design by Sharon Bartsch
Back cover design by Dave Hauser
Interior designed by Dave Hauser
Edited by Kristine Manty

Printed in China

DEDICATION

for Alex

And to my families:

Mom, Dad, Christie, Amber, Jeremy, Brian, and their families

and

Nicholas, Travis, and Rebecca.

Without everyone, this book would not have been possible.

ACKNOWLEDGMENTS

Special thanks to Sylvester Stallone for making *Rambo IV* and inspiring me to create a little website that has led to so many other great things. Thank you to Brett Reno, a.k.a Rick Swift, for all his support from the very beginning. And thanks to all of my other friends, both online and off, as well as my Twitter army, who have always been more than willing to answer my random questions and talk about action movies with me.

Also thanks to Heritage Auctions (www.ha.com) and The Picture Desk (www.picture-desk.com), the online home of The Kobal Collection, for the photos used in this book.

CONTENTS

Action Movies: Explode, Rinse, Repeat

Action movies! Some say they're devoid of any thought-provoking plot or deep character growth. Some say that action movies are only for adrenaline junkies who want to get a rush. And to them I say, "Hell yeah they are—that's why I love them!" Action movies are a hot-and-heavy-get-your-blood-pumping-watching-bad-guys-get-their-blood-pumped-onto-the-walls kind of fun!

Now, that doesn't mean people who watch action movies are any less thoughtful than people who watch foofy shmooffy romance movies or cerebrally oriented, Oscar-winning films. Not all action movies are completely devoid of plot, and not everyone who loves action movies is an adrenaline junkie. We're just fun-loving people who want to see things get blown up in a safe environment. After all, it's not everyday that someone's walking down the street and gets to see Spider-Man swinging from building to building saving people from muggers, or see a divorced father with a special set of skills take down a human trafficking organization by himself because they kidnapped his daughter, or see a veteran take out an entire platoon of soldiers using a red bandana and bow and arrow.

In fact, I, personally, have never seen any of that happening in real life, which is a rather good thing when you stop to think about it.

So what am I saying? I'm saying that action movies are awesome! And they serve an important function in society: escapism. If I wanted to experience deep, meaningful, thought-provoking conversations, I'd turn the TV off, go outside and have one with the squirrels. When I sit down to watch a film, I want to see something different. I want to watch Chuck Norris round house kick someone in the face for no reason! There's a time and place for everything, and according to my clock, it's always time for action.

Who This Book is For

Action Movie Freak is for everyone, whether you love action movies or not. If you're thinking, "I hate action movies, why would I want to read this book?" Here's why: Reading this book will educate you on all the essential action movies so you'll never have to watch one again ... and/or maybe this book will convince you that action movies are fantastic entertainment and convert you into an action movie freak.

Now, if you already are an action movie freak, this book will just remind you of why action films are amazing and hopefully make you think back to the good times you had sneaking into the living room to watch *RoboCop* with your dad even though your mom told you not to. *Action Movie Freak* is a guide celebrating years of films high in adrenaline and fun.

The Essence of an Action Movie

There are certain qualities that make up a good action movie. Believe it or not, not all action is good. It's like a hamburger. Sure,

Arnold Schwarzenegger and Sylvester Stallone play bare-chested heroes that action freaks can always get behind. Here they are as John Matrix in *Commando* and Rambo in *Rambo II*.
Top: 20th Century Fox/Heritage Auctions; bottom: Anabasis Investments/Heritage Auctions

cheese, beef, and a bun together can be good, but an unskilled hamburger cook might just throw them all in a blender and say, "Here. Chug this crap." You have to take the right ingredients and cook them just so to come out with something tasty, starting with:

1. The Hero/Heroine: A vast majority of what will determine if an action movie is a good one or not is the lead character. First and foremost the lead has to be likeable in some way, giving a foundation to build the rest of the story on. If the audience doesn't like them, they'll probably be rooting for the hero to perish instead of the bad guys.

A good hero/heroine should be able to kick some major ass, too! Whether it's by having mad martial art skills, expert gun slinging skills, or exceptional brain power and outsmarting the opposing force, a good lead character will pull some amazing tricks and do whatever it takes to get a job done.

They should also be willing to risk it all for the sake of their mission. Even though they might be killing people (hopefully people who are well established as bad guys), they're risking their own lives for the mission. For example, in *Rambo (IV)*, Rambo doesn't have to go into Burma to save the missionaries being held there. After all, he doesn't know them; he owes them nothing. But he does it anyway, because he's a good person at heart, and because he's freaking Rambo!

Lastly, a lead character with a snarky wit isn't required, but goes a long, long way toward making a likable character and good movie.

Audiences love to hate villains like Hans Gruber (Alan Rickman) in *Die Hard*.
20th Century Fox/The Kobal Collection

2. The Villain: As much as the hero should be loved, the villain (or baddies as I often refer to them as) should be hated. What makes people love to hate villains like Hans Gruber and T-1000 is that they don't care who they hurt. Whether it's men, women, children, the elderly, or mimes, they do it because it'd be inconvenient not to, and sometimes because they like it. Great villains should be like a black hole in the film—unstoppable gravitational forces that pull everything around them into conflict until something gives or explodes.

3. The Mission: Why is the hero/ heroine doing what they're doing? No matter what happens, the lead character's actions should be working toward something the viewer can care

In *Kill Bill,* the mission of the The Bride (Uma Thurman) is to get revenge on the people responsible for killing everyone near and dear to her.
A Band Apart/Miramax/The Kobal Collection

Chuck Norris running after someone in *Missing in Action* is good action. Chuck Norris kicking the ass of that someone after catching him is *great* action.
Cannon/The Kobal Collection

Turning yourself into a full-metal killing machine and leaving a pile of dead Reavers on the floor, as River Tam (Summer Glau) does in *Serenity*, is AWESOME action. Universal Studios

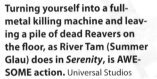

If it weren't for stunt people putting themselves on the line for action movies, there would be no Evel Knievel-style flying out windows, like in this scene from *Terminator 2.* Carolco/The Kobal Collection

about. Of course, what the viewer cares about differs from person to person, but there are some common themes, like love, justice, and making sure that there's enough beer in the fridge.

4. The Amount of Action: The amount of action will make a difference in how well a film is liked, especially if the first three categories are lacking. A film can sometimes get away with one-

dimensional heroes and villains, and even a plot so threadbare it's almost nonexistent, so long as there's enough action to keep everything moving and the viewer distracted. Action is best when applied early, spread evenly throughout the film, baked for an hour, and ends in a huge explosion of a finale.

5. The Quality of Action: As said before, not all action equals good action. Technically, action can be anything done or performed. Walking is an action, but that's not exciting unless it's Jason Statham in *Power Walking 2: Deathwalk* (which isn't real but I wish it was). Since walking is a baseline action that most everyone does, an action movie needs to go above and beyond that, bringing loads of energy and intensity to what's going on. Good, high-quality action is something not everyone can pull off, and the more realistic it looks the better. Someone running after a purse thief is action. Someone pushing past people and climbing fences to catch the purse thief is good action. Someone running through an amusement park and ending the chase in a brawl atop a moving rollercoaster … well, that's awesome action, the kind that would be in *Power Walking 2*. Like a song, sometimes it's not about what's being said in an action sequence, it's about how it's being said.

6. The Stunts. Stunt people are the folks putting their bodies and lives on the line to bring us entertainment. They do the dangerous stuff. The awesome, "Oh my God did someone actually do that?" stuff so that the actors can keep their pretty faces looking pretty and so that the film has something exciting in it. And they do it all while keeping their faces hidden beneath a helmet or a pile of hair. There wouldn't be many action stars left or people willing to make action movies if it weren't for the stunt people. So to those brave stunt teams everywhere, I say bravo, and thank you!

And there you have it. These six things are some of the most crucial ingredients in an action movie. When cooked right, they'll sizzle and satisfy. When prepared poorly, they'll leave you bored and diarrhea stricken. That's why action movies are like Happy Meals, but for grownups! They're fun, make you happy, and give you something to think back on and get excited about. Like the action genre itself, there are many different ingredients that come together to form a Happy Meal, first and foremost of which is a good old-fashioned hamburger.

While actors keep their pretty faces, stunt people risk life and limb, and even set themselves on fire, in this scene from *Predator*. 20th Century Fox/Heritage Auctions

THE HAMBURGER

Classic Action Movies

Let's start building that Happy Meal, beginning with the hamburger. What are the basics needed to make a hamburger? Gotta have some meat and a bun, otherwise the burger is just a weird salad with ketchup on it. Likewise, the classic action movies are the meat and the bun of the action genre—they provide a good foundation as well as something meaty to sink your teeth into!

A classic film sets a standard which all other movies should strive to meet; it's the paragon of perfect action-itude. Classics have the significance to inspire the viewers of today to make the movies of tomorrow, and the ass-kickingness to withstand the test of time. After all, classics are the kind of films that veteran action movie freaks keep coming back to over and over again, the ones older siblings show to their way too young brother or sister even though they're not supposed to.

Even though most of the classics are several decades old, they've still got enough muscles, mayhem, and swagger to get the blood pumping of all action movie freaks, young and old alike.

Sam Peckinpah's 1969 western, *The Wild Bunch*, was controversial for its time because of its unflinching graphic violence. Warner 7 Arts/Heritage Auctions

300

DIRECTED BY Zack Snyder
WRITTEN BY Zack Snyder (screenplay), Kurt Johnstad (screenplay), Michael Gordon (screenplay), Frank Miller (graphic novel), Lynn Varley (graphic novel)
STARRING Gerard Butler, Lena Headey, David Wenham
RELEASED March 9, 2007
RATED R

Sometimes you feel like a nut, and sometimes you don't. Sometimes you feel like watching a movie that's so overflowing with testosterone that Hazmat suits are needed lest you break out in body hair from over-exposure, and sometimes you feel like watching a little orange fish swim around in the ocean making friends with sharks and turtles. When the desire to watch the former occurs, suit up and turn on *300*!

Xerxes (Rodrigo Santoro), the king of Persia with delusions of deityhood, has been rampaging a massive army across the globe, demanding that any who oppose him submit to his rule or be destroyed. Freedom is on the verge of extinction, forcing Spartan King Leonidas (Gerard Butler) to finally step up to tell Xerxes to kiss his muscular Greek ass! Spartans never surrender and Spartans never retreat!

It's unfortunate, then, that the Persian messenger sent to Sparta doesn't know that bit of info. He certainly learned it the hard way when King Leonidas shouts the most memorable line from *300*, "This is Sparta!" and kicks that Xerxes-loving messenger into a pit of death.

Xerxes' looming threat ignites a fire in King Leonidas, who "goes for a walk" with 300 of his best soldiers while secretly planning to fight the army of one million in what has become known as the Battle of Thermopylae.

300 is derived from the comic series of the same name, which is loosely based on a true historical happening of the real King Leonidas taking a small army of approximately 300 Spartans and meeting up with a few hundred more from other places to take on tens of thousands of Persians. When it comes to action movie badasses, this guy is the true king of them all—he isn't just a character in a movie; he lived by the sword, and he died by it.

Visually, *300* might be one of the most uniquely scintillating films

PERSIAN:
"A thousand nations of the Persian Empire descend upon you. Our arrows will blot out the sun!"

STELIOS:
"Then we will fight in the shade."

Rather than focus on historical accuracy, director Zack Snyder chose instead to make a movie heavy on excitement and visually stunning action.
Warner Bros./Legendary Pictures/The Kobal Collection

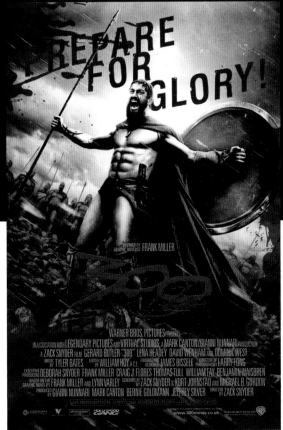

Warner Bros./Legendary Pictures

to come out of Hollywood in a long time. Zack Snyder loves to make a splash, and he absolutely succeeded with this film. The boldly colored scenery, the ridiculously ripped men, and stylish use of slow-motion in the action sequences all work together to create a moving portrait of carnage in every action sequence.

Warning: it should be known that watching *300* makes a person 300 percent more likely to run around kicking things over, all the while screaming those three magic words ...

"THIS IS SPARTA!"

Seven Samurai

DIRECTED BY Akira Kurosawa
WRITTEN BY Akira Kurosawa, Shinobu Hashimoto, Hideo Oguni
STARRING Toshirô Mifune, Takashi Shimura, Keiko Tsushima
RELEASED April 26, 1954
UNRATED

Seven versus forty. Whether you're talking about men, dogs, or action figures, seven versus forty would usually be an impossible match for the seven to win, but not when they have brains, balls of steel, and the best sword-wielding men in the country. That's exactly who the men are in *Seven Samurai,* and they're not interested in playing with action figures—they're out for *blood*. The same goes for the seven men in *The Magnificent Seven,* only their weapons of choice are guns instead of swords.

GISAKU:

"What's the use of worrying about your beard when your head's about to be taken?"

When you have brains and balls of steel, not to mention wicked sword-wielding skills, seven of you is all it takes to defeat a small army. Toho/Heritage Auctions

Toho/Heritage Auctions

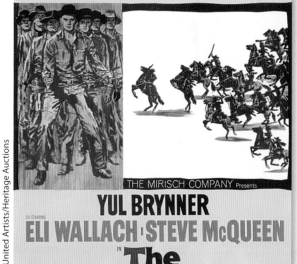

DIRECTED BY John Sturges
WRITTEN BY William Roberts (screenplay), Walter Bernstein (uncredited), Walter Newman (uncredited)
STARRING Yul Brenner, Steve McQueen, Charles Bronson, Eli Wallach, Robert Vaughn, Brad Dexter, James Coburn
RELEASED October 23, 1960
RATED PG

Seven Samurai became so influential in the U.S. that the American version, *The Magnificent Seven,* was made and quickly became a classic alongside the original. The basic plot doesn't differ between the two films: a village of farmers hires seven men to protect them from bandits who annually swarm their village like locusts and take their food, leaving them to subsist on barely anything.

For an adventure film from 1954, the action in *Seven Samurai* is legendary. There's plenty of wonderfully choreographed stunts between the horseback riding and sword play that had never been done before. *The Magnificent Seven* takes its cue from *Seven Samurai's* state of the art sword swinging action and converts it

into a gun-slinging exhibition.

Both movies aren't just "action" films, though, as they came from a time before "action" movies as we know them existed. These films have a bit more philosophy behind them, diving into how lonely and unfulfilling the life of a wandering hero can be. In fact, one of the best things about these two movies is the character development of these manly men.

These films may not hold up in terms of action against the modern action movie where "more bullets + more blood = more better," but they're still great movies with impressive stunts and a plotline that transcends time and society. The story of a group of men facing certain destruction, and a lone hero with a will of steel gathering up this rogue's gallery, is a tale that's been retold countless times. Even modern stories like *Ironclad* or *Seven Samurai 20XX* can all be traced back to Akira Kurosawa's original work. Plus seeing seven good guys take out forty bad guys can always get a person pumped up!

BRITT:
"Nobody throws me my own guns and says run. Nobody."

Each of the Magnificent Seven has a different reason for agreeing to help a Mexican village fend off bandits. United Artists/The Kobal Collection.

You can always count on Joss Whedon to produce greatness. When called in to doctor the script for *Speed* and make the lead character Jack Tavern (Keanu Reeves) more believable, less cliché, and frankly just less of an overall wang, Whedon waved his magic JossWand™ and helped create one of the most financially and critically successful action movies of its time.

Howard Payne (Dennis Hopper), a pissed off retired police officer, decides to earn his retirement fund by planting bombs on a couple of buses and then demanding ransom in exchange for not blowing them up. SWAT team member Jack Tavern races to action after witnessing one bus explode in a hailstorm of flames and metal. He boards another bus only to find that it, too, has a bomb and a Sandra Bullock, and that this bus will also explode if it drops below 50 miles per hour. What to do, what to do.

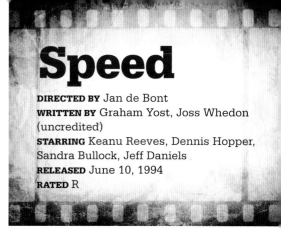

Speed

DIRECTED BY Jan de Bont
WRITTEN BY Graham Yost, Joss Whedon (uncredited)
STARRING Keanu Reeves, Dennis Hopper, Sandra Bullock, Jeff Daniels
RELEASED June 10, 1994
RATED R

Keanu Reeves and Sandra Bullock try to keep a bus flying down a busy LA freeway above 50 miles per hour or everyone will get blown to smithereens.
20th Century Fox/The Kobal Collection/Richard Foreman

"Harry, there's enough C-4 on this thing to put a hole in the world."

Speed is a superb mix of high-speed action, likeable characters, and a well-paced story, all of which combine to make it an instant classic. In fact, *Speed* is so intense that viewers will grip tight and probably crush anything they can get their hands on while watching it, so it's probably best to hide any breakables during the first viewing, including, but not limited to, cups, TV remotes, and any pets and/or children.

Sometimes a film has to work hard to keep the tension up, as the story might not lend itself toward being the high-octane thrill ride the director wants it to be. Well, *Speed* sure doesn't have that problem, because there are few things more balls-out nuts than trying to keep a bus flying down a busy LA highway at fifty-plus miles per hour. Throw in a psychotic villain willing to blow up anyone who so much as *thinks* about trying to move against his master plan and you're left feeling like anything could happen.

As far as classic action films go, *Speed* is an obvious gold mine. Its sequel, however, is considered one of the worst sequels of all time, so if it's playing, you might want to *speed* off in the other direction.

Special Mention for Top Action Scene:
Point Break

A special recognition goes to *Point Break* for having a memorable, crazy action scene. Police officer Utah (Keanu Reeves) thinks he's finally busted bank robber Bodhi (Patrick Swayze) in an airplane. There's nowhere to escape in an airplane, right? WRONG. Bodhi jumps out of the plane with a parachute, and rather than lose track of the criminal, Utah jumps out of the plane as well … sans parachute! There's approximately 90 seconds of nail-biting suspense as they freefall. Utah finally catches up to Bodhi and fastens on to him. Then, as if that wasn't enough to get the heart pumping, they play a game of chicken when Bodhi refuses to pull the rip cord, forcing Utah into deciding whether he wants to keep his gun (and prisoner) or pull the cord and save both of their lives. At the very last second, Utah drops the gun and pulls the rip cord, saving them both from an untimely, splattery demise.

Reeves and Swayze catchng some Gs in a nail-biting scene. 20th Century Fox

Dirty Harry Series Retrospective

Harry Callahan: Making criminals poop their pants since 1971! Dirty Harry is one of Clint Eastwood's most iconic roles: a smart, tough-as-nails cop who will do what it takes to make certain justice gets served. He's skilled, he's confident, and he has enough badass swagger to make every man, woman, and beast know he means business. Even inanimate objects cower in terror when they hear those five foreboding words …"Go ahead, make my day." Has anyone ever gotten a chance to make Dirty Harry's day? Once he's pointing his Smith & Wesson .44 Magnum at a criminal, most of them probably don't want to take the chance.

Dirty Harry set up precedent for the many movie cops and action heroes who followed him in his unwavering pursuit of justice, even if it comes at the price of bending the rules for the greater good. Without him, we probably wouldn't have the *Lethal Weapon* series, or the Italian Poliziotteschi films, or the *Judge Dredd* movie. Okay, so maybe we'd be better off without *Judge Dredd*, but the rest of those are great movies!

There are five films in the *Dirty Harry* series, each following a similar pattern with different foes cut and pasted in. First, most of the films begin with D.H. reminding viewers of what a badass he is by single handedly taking down some random thugs. After that, he'll probably be reprimanded by a superior officer for being such a "loose cannon" and "not following the rules." He may even get suspended and/or get a new partner, not that it matters. In the end, he'll still single handedly take down the lead antagonist, and he'll do it with the kind of heroic menace you just can't buy.

Dirty Harry

DIRECTED BY Don Siegel
WRITTEN BY Harry Julian Fink (story/screenplay), & Rita M. Fink (story/screenplay), Dean Riesner (screenplay), John Milius (screenplay) uncredited, and Jo Heims story (uncredited)
STARRING Clint Eastwood, Andrew Robinson, John Vernon
RELEASED Dec. 23, 1971
RATED R

The first of the series, *Dirty Harry*, is about a mysterious murderer codenamed Scorpio, a sniper who kills his victims from rooftops before moving on to kidnappings and ransom demands. Enter Dirty Harry.

This film is sort of lacking in the action department but it *does* introduce Harry Callahan and tells why he's called "Dirty" Harry: "I take every dirty job that comes along." Regardless, just having Harry in a film ups its action badassery 100 percent.

HARRY CALLAHAN:
"Now you know why they call me Dirty Harry… every dirty job that comes along."

Harry delivers his famous speech, all while squinting and wearing a snazzy suit. Warner Bros./Heritage Auctions

Dirty Harry is also the origin of the famous speech quoted by many even today. Imagine staring down the barrel of Harry's gun when he says:

"I know what you're thinking. 'Did he fire six shots or only five?' Well, to tell you the truth, in all this excitement I kind of lost track myself. But being as this is a .44 Magnum, the most powerful handgun in the world, and would blow your head clean off, you've got to ask yourself one question: Do I feel lucky? Well, do ya, punk?"

It's an incredibly famous line; so much so that it's been repeated and parodied in everything from Jim Carrey's *The Mask* to Michelle Yeoh's *Yes, Madam*.

At left is an example of Harry "playing by the rules." He just pulled a suicidal man off of the ledge rather than taking him down. Warner Bros./Heritage Auctions

Magnum Force

DIRECTED BY Ted Post
WRITTEN BY Harry Jilian Fink (original material), Rita M. Fink (original material), John Milius (screenplay and story), Michael Cimino (screenplay)
STARRING Clint Eastwood, Hal Holbrook, Mitch Ryan
RELEASED Dec. 25, 1973
RATED R

Next, Harry takes on vigilante cops who are tracking down and killing criminals that have somehow escaped the judicial system. You might think Harry would be one of them, seeing as how he often crosses lines and "forgets" to play by the books just to catch a villain, but in the end it's that never-ending pursuit of justice that sets him apart as a good cop. The theme of *Magnum Force* can be summed up by Harry, "A good man always knows his limitations."

HARRY CALLAHAN:
"This is a .44 Magnum, the most powerful handgun in the world, and it could blow your head clean off. Do you feel lucky?"

Corpses, carnage, and bloodshed ... just another day on the job for Dirty Harry.
Columbia/Warner Bros./Heritage Auctions

Two people who are not Dirty Harry do things that are decidedly less badass than what Harry would have done. Warner Bros./Heritage Auctions

Harry doesn't take kindly to certain people. Well, actually to most anyone.
Warner Bros./Heritage Auctions

The Enforcer

DIRECTED BY James Fargo
WRITTEN BY Harry Julian Fink (original material), Rita M. Fink (original material), Stirling Silliphant (screenplay), Dean Riesner (screenplay), Gail Morgan Hickman (story), S.W. Schurr (story)
STARRING Clint Eastwood, Tyne Daly, Harry Guardino
RELEASED Dec. 22, 1976
RATED R

In the third installment, *The Enforcer,* Dirty Harry goes up against a terrorist group calling themselves The People's Revolutionary Strike Force, which is not the catchiest name for a terrorist group, but whatever. I especially like the scene at the beginning of this flick—some thugs have taken hostages inside a store and are demanding a car. When asked what Harry's going to do, he says, "Give them one," then drives his freakin' car through the glass door into the store, right before hopping out and blowing the thugs to bits. Dirty Harry: problem solver!

KATE MOORE:

"You laugh at me, you bastard, and I'll shoot you where you stand."

Sudden Impact

DIRECTED BY Clint Eastwood
WRITTEN BY Harry Julian Fink (original material), Rita M. Fink (original material), Joseph Stinson (screenplay), Earl E. Smith (story), Charles B. Pierce (story)
STARRING Clint Eastwood, Sondra Locke, Pat Hingle
RELEASED Dec. 9, 1983
RATED R

"Go ahead, make my day."

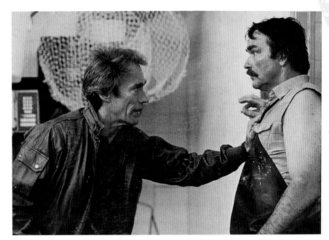

The action in *Sudden Impact* is faster paced than in the previous movies. Warner Bros./Malpaso/Heritage Auctions

Sudden Impact, my favorite of the series, follows a rape victim getting revenge on the perpetrators and their junk. Can Dirty Harry figure out who's killing all these men in time to save them? Or does he even want to? The real question Dirty Harry has to figure out is: who is the real bad guy here? The woman getting revenge or the rapists?

The action in this film is top-notch; much faster paced than the previous *Dirty Harry* films. Someone is constantly trying to attack Harry, and it always results in some kind of car chase, bomb, and/or gunfight. The higher frequency of action also means a higher frequency of DH quips, including the birth of one of his most iconic lines: "Go ahead, make my day." The film climaxes in a brilliant, wordless showdown where Harry faces down the villains and takes them out without a single word being exchanged between the two sides. At that point, nothing they could say would've helped, anyway, because once Harry shows up with that look in his eye, it's clear that the morgue is going to be getting some new tenants.

Sondra Locke is a rape victim seeking revenge. Warner Bros./Malpaso/Heritage Auctions

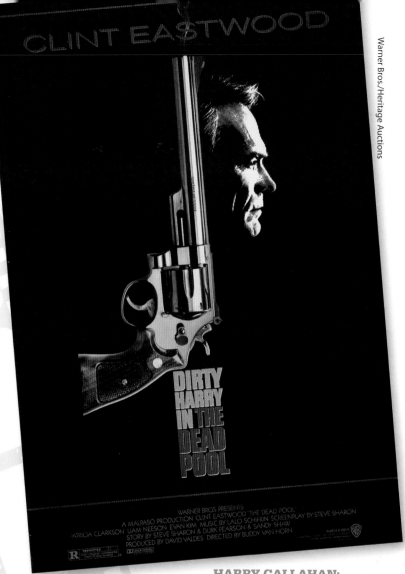

HARRY CALLAHAN:
"Do you have any kids, lieutenant?"

LT. ACKERMAN:
"Me? No."

HARRY CALLAHAN:
"Lucky for them."

The Dead Pool

DIRECTED BY Buddy Van Horn
WRITTEN BY Harry Julian Fink (original material), Rita M. Fink (original material), Steve Sharon (story/screenplay), Durk Pearson (story), Sandy Shaw (story)
STARRING Clint Eastwood, Liam Neeson, Patricia Clarkson
RELEASED July 13, 1988
RATED R

After spending the first four movies blowing away endless waves of bad guys, Dirty Harry's got the remaining baddies kind of riled up and coming at him from all directions in *The Dead Pool.* This time he finds himself as a target of a contest where people bet on which celebrity will die next. Between people involved in the dead pool trying to kill him and the everyday criminals who have it out for Harry, he's constantly beating the puke out of someone. While not the best of the series, there is a small treat in this film that the others don't have: a young Jim Carrey!

Even though the *Dirty Harry* series isn't, overall, the most action-packed of films, there's still a smorgasbord of goodness for action lovers to feast on, and most of that is Dirty Harry himself. He's one of the most iconic characters in film history, and with good reason. He's tough, he's tireless, and knows exactly the right thing to say right before he shoots a criminal between the eyes. Since he's such a font of great one liners, I'll leave you with a friendly reminder he spouted in *The Dead Pool*: "Well, opinions are like assholes. Everyone has one."

The Killer

DIRECTED/WRITEN BY John Woo
STARRING Chow Yun-Fat, Danny Lee, Sally Yeh
RELEASED September 1990 (USA)
UNRATED

Wherever Ah Jong (Chow Yun-Fat) goes, a trail of dead bodies seems to follow. To be fair, though, in *The Killer* he isn't the one always picking the fight despite being an assassin. In a move typical of most movie assassins, Ah Jong grows a conscience and tries to turn his life around. Too bad he decides to do this just one damn day too late.

During one assignment, Ah Jong accidentally damages the eyes of a singer in the restaurant, leaving her mostly blind. With guilt gnawing at him like a zombie, he watches her from a distance until they eventually "meet" and become an item. Ah Jong takes one last assignment to earn enough money to fix his lady's eyesight, but accidentally reveals his identity to police officer Li Ying (Danny Lee).

Since Ah Jong works for the Triad and they aren't big on having their assassins getting buddy-buddy with the cops, they decide that it's time for Ah Jong to go to the Great Wall in the Sky. Li Ying becomes mixed up in the shenanigans as he becomes obsessed with arresting Ah Jong and ultimately teams up with him to help in his battle against The Triad.

Ah Jong should get an award for most

times to be shot at without injury because this dude always has bullets flying at him from all directions but manages to evade virtually every one of them. Maybe a lot of that can be contributed to the usual style of gunfights John Woo always has in his films where everyone either falls or jumps onto their sides as they're shooting. That can't possibly help you aim, people!

The film really focuses on the theme of brotherhood between Jong and Li Ying; even though these two are on opposite teams, so to speak, they have a common moral code that unites them. *The Killer* is full of elements common to John Woo films: the slow-motion, the leaping-sideways-while-shooting, the freaking doves, but it's this

touch of humanity between Jong and Li Ying that raises the stakes on what might otherwise be a typical John Woo bullet-fest.

AH JONG:
"I always leave one bullet, either for myself or for my enemy."

The Killer's **original title?** *Squinting and Shooting.* Film Workshop/The Kobal Collection

개같이 살기보단 英雄처럼 죽고싶다!

喋血双雄

THE KILLER

주윤발 VS 이수현 엽천문 증강 각본 감독 오우삼

Film Workshop

27

The Wild Bunch

DIRECTED BY Sam Peckinpah
WRITTEN BY Walon Green (screenplay/story), Sam Peckinpah (screenplay), Roy N. Sickner (story)
STARRING William Holden, Ernest Borgnine, Robert Ryan
RELEASED June 18, 1969
RATED R

In a time when the horror of the Vietnam War was plaguing America, *The Wild Bunch*'s stark portrayals of violence stirred mixed emotions across the country. Some critics found it too violent, while others enjoyed the symbolism of the harsh realities of war.

For any action movie freak, however, hearing that a movie is too violent is like hearing that there's too much hot fudge in an ice cream sundae. It's absurd! Nonetheless, whether it was being talked about positively or negatively, *The Wild Bunch* became well known for its realistic look at the often violent, always wild, old west.

The story of *The Wild Bunch* centers on a group of aging outlaws led by Pike

Unchanged men in a changing land.
Out of step, out of place and desperately out of time.

A PHIL FELDMAN PRODUCTION

THE WILD BUNCH

WILLIAM HOLDEN · ERNEST BORGNINE · ROBERT RYAN · EDMOND O'BRIEN · WARREN OATES · JAIME SANCHEZ · BEN JOHNSON

ALSO STARRING EMILIO FERNANDEZ · STROTHER MARTIN · L. Q. JONES · Screenplay by WALON GREEN and SAM PECKINPAH · Music by Jerry Fielding · Story by Walon Green and Roy N. Sickner · Produced by PHIL FELDMAN · Directed by SAM PECKINPAH · TECHNICOLOR® PANAVISION® FROM WARNER BROS.-SEVEN ARTS

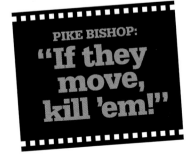

PIKE BISHOP:
"If they move, kill 'em!"

Bishop (William Holden) looking to score one last robbery to retire on. Things go awry (as they often do on these pre-retirement heists) when their plans are foiled by an old friend/partner, Deke Thornton (Robert Ryan). Licking their wounds after the betrayal, the group decides to see if they fare better in Mexico and end up taking a dangerous new job from a Mexican general.

The American Film Institute named *The Wild Bunch* as the sixth

Dutch (Borgnine) and Pike (Holden) in a bloody showdown. Warner 7 Arts/Heritage Auctions

best western, 80th in the "100 Best American films," and 69th in the "Most Thrilling" film category. It was picked for preservation by the Library of Congress and nominated for many awards. There's only one explanation as to why this film has received so many acknowledgments: it freakin' rocks! *The Wild Bunch* was one of the first films for its time to show such graphic material and employ modern action techniques, such as slow-motion shots and intricate breakdowns of the onscreen action, all of which were revolutionary techniques in 1969.

Another element of the film that was revolutionary for its time is just how *brutal* it is. Even when compared to modern action movies, *The Wild Bunch* is like a hairy, abusive, drunken grandmother. It's loud, it's violent, and it's not afraid to go places that most politically correct films won't. Children and women are getting gunned down as well as gunning a few people down themselves. At one point, Pike uses a woman as a shield from incoming enemy bullets. And *that* guy is the freaking hero! That was the goal of writer/director Sam Peckinpah: he had become so frustrated by the lack of reality in western films and the violence so many Americans were suffering through at that time, that he wanted to portray such cruelty with a stark realism.

Foxy Brown

DIRECTED/WRITTEN BY Jack Hill
STARRING Pam Grier, Antonio Fargas, Peter Brown, Terry Carter
RELEASED April 5, 1974
RATED R

While most exploitation films may not have action as the primary focus, it doesn't change the fact that they often have plenty, and it's usually really freakin' violent. That's what the films are made for, right? To exploit certain things, like violence and nudity, and exploit they do.

A classic film from the blaxploitation genre is *Foxy Brown.* In it, Pam Grier plays the infamous Foxy Brown, a tough-as-nails lady out for revenge after mobsters murder her boyfriend and she gets kidnapped and put through hell. She's a tenacious chick, though, and makes the best of a bad situation by breaking out and killing all of the men holding her hostage, some of whom meet their demise in brutal and dastardly ways.

Foxy Brown is one of the most culturally significant blaxploitation films ever made, with a legacy that extends far beyond the film itself. Some of that may be due to it being one of the first blaxploitation films to show a woman as strong and independent from men, not a hostage who counts on guys to come take care of things when it gets too rough.

She's also smart and so full of sass you'll probably contract type-1 sassiness just from being around her. I haven't heard anyone be able to say "bitch" with as much attitude as Foxy does.

Action movie freaks looking for a classic blaxploitation film, filled with awesome 'fros and a brutal story of revenge should watch *Foxy Brown.* There's plenty of exploitation to be found, as well as a heaping helping of violence and, the cherry on top: one confident, take-charge heroine.

> MICHAEL ANDERSON:
> ## "I don't know ... vigilante justice?"
> FOXY BROWN:
> ## "It's as American as apple pie."

Take-charge Foxy Brown dispenses vigilante justice her way. AIP/The Kobal Collection

PAM GRIER

Pam Grier is one hell of a lady. As the first African-American woman to star in an action film, she helped create and shape the action heroines of today, and her ability to portray women of unbreakable spirit set the path for more women to take on leading roles and more writers to create those types of roles.

Pam Grier, in a scene from *Foxy Brown*, helped shape the action heroines of today. AIP/The Kobal Collection

She first made a name for herself by starring in blaxploitation and "women in prison" films. Her first roles had her working with Roger Corman in the Philippines on *The Big Doll House* and *The Big Bird Cage*. *Machete Maidens Unleashed!*, a documentary on the terrible working conditions moviemakers had to endure when filming in the Philippines, definitely shows what a real-life heroine Grier is for coming out of there alive and still wanting to make movies.

After such exceptional displays of strength shown in her early works, Grier went on to become a leading lady of action in films such as *Coffy*, *Foxy Brown*, and *Friday Foster*. She even played partner to Steven Seagal in *Above the Law*, but her most famous role, however, may be Quentin Tarantino's *Jackie Brown*, where she portrays a flight attendant who manages to pull one over on the cops and a gun runner at the same time.

Grier possesses the ability to play action characters with a little bit of pizzazz and a whole lot of tenacity, instantly making her an action heroine favorite and a role model for writers and women everywhere.

Bullitt

DIRECTED BY Peter Yates
WRITTEN BY Alan Trustman (screenplay), Harry Kleiner (screenplay), Robert L. Fish (novel, Mute Witness)
STARRING Steve McQueen, Jacqueline Bisset, Robert Vaughn
RELEASED October 17, 1968
RATED PG

If an action movie freak is looking for one of the best car chase scenes in cinema history, Bullitt is where you'll find it. The chase scene was so popular that the Ford Mustang, the car used for the scene, became famous for it and is still referred to as the *Bullitt* car. So take a trip back to 1968 and enjoy some high-octane racing!

Lieutenant Frank Bullitt (Steve McQueen) has been assigned to protect a key witness that politician, Chalmers (Robert Vaughn), intends to use to take down a Chicago mob boss and better his standings in the political world. Bullitt goes from protective duty to being the lead investigator on a Sunday after his key witness dies from a gunshot wound. His boss gives him until Monday to solve the case, meaning Bullitt has to get his ass in gear if he's ever going to figure out who killed his key witness and how.

As stated earlier, *Bullitt* is responsible for one of the most influential car chase scenes in history, a scene so famous it was listed in *Time* magazine's list of "The 15 Greatest Movie Car Chases of All Time." The scene runs

BULLITT:
"Look, you work your side of the street, and I'll work mine."

Although *Bullitt* is known for its car chase scene through the streets of San Francisco, action takes place at the airport, too. Warner Bros./Heritage Auctions

Steve McQueen gives a powerhouse performance as title character Frank Bullitt.
Warner Bros./Heritage Auctions

The word 'cop' isn't written all over him— something more puzzling is.

STEVE McQUEEN AS 'BULLITT'
ROBERT VAUGHN

CO-STARRING JACQUELINE BISSET · DON GORDON · ROBERT DUVALL · SIMON OAKLAND · NORMAN FELL

A SOLAR PRODUCTION

Music by Lalo Schifrin · Screenplay by ALAN R. TRUSTMAN and HARRY KLEINER · Based on the novel "Mute Witness" by Robert L. Pike · Directed by PETER YATES · Produced by PHILIP D'ANTONI · Executive Producer ROBERT E. RELYEA

TECHNICOLOR® FROM WARNER BROS.-SEVEN ARTS

M SUGGESTED FOR MATURE AUDIENCES

Copyright © 1968 Warner Bros.-Seven Arts, Inc. Printed in U.S.A.

almost 11 minutes long, with Bullitt chasing two hit men in Ford Mustangs, and incorporated the cars ramping up and down the hills of San Francisco. The director utilized a camera from the driver's point of view to really give the audience the feeling of being in the car, experiencing the chase first-hand. The chase ends in the best way possible: an explosion! It became the perfect example as soon as it was released.

Bullitt, as a whole, is a technically impressive film. It's won awards not just for the chase scene but for editing, cinematography, and directing. And let's not forget a powerhouse performance from the always-extraordinary Steve McQueen.

Charlie's Angels

DIRECTED BY McG
WRITTEN BY Ryan Rowe (screenplay/story/characters), Ed Solomon (screenplay/story/characters), John August (screenplay/story/characters), Ivan Goff (TV series), Ben Roberts (TV series)
STARRING Drew Barrymore, Cameron Diaz, Lucy Liu
RELEASED November 3, 2000
RATED PG-13

Not many people can make "flip your god damn hair" sound like a serious threat, but Lucy Liu pulls it off with finesse in *Charlie's Angels*. Based on the '70s TV show of the same name, this modern movie features three attractive, highly capable private investigators who don disguises and bust out some martial arts to get the job done. And they've got Bill Murray with them, too. Interested yet?

Charlie's Angels originally got its start as a television show in 1976. Later, as an effort to revive the franchise, two feature films were made. In the first one, private investigators Natalie Cook (Cameron Diaz), Dylan Sanders (Drew Barrymore), and Alex Munday (Lucy Liu) are called in to find a kidnapped Eric Knox (Sam Rockwell), a computer programmer and creator of voice recognition software. The Angels have no problem finding and rescuing him. In fact, it was a little too easy, and they soon find out why. It seems that Knox set the whole thing up so that he could use his voice recognition program to find Charlie, the Angels' unseen

VIVIAN WOOD:

"Never send a man to do a woman's job."

employer, as Knox believes Charlie was responsible for his father's death and he's hungry for some good old fashioned revenge. So now the Angels must stop Knox before he kills Charlie and leaves them unemployed.

This film is an action comedy if I've ever seen one, filled with light-hearted and often corny moments, as well as Bill "Bustin' Makes Me Feel Good" Murray, who serves as the comedic relief. As far as the action half of the movie goes, the Angels are stupendous warriors, using both their minds and physical skills in some outlandish wire-

fu style fight scenes. The stunt work is impressive, including an array of driving stunts, explosions, and a sky-diving scene reminiscent of Point Break (featuring LL Cool J. Confused? Me, too).

The lack of concern for realism, brief moments of titillation, and frequent bouts of cornball comedy make *Charlie's Angels* an excellent choice for anyone feeling nostalgic for their adolescent days, where all it took was a good ass joke to make you giggle, or a fist-fight with a creepy thin man to get you pumped.

If the theme from *Charlie's Angels* isn't going through your head right now, something's wrong. Columbia/The Kobal Collection/Darren Michaels

35

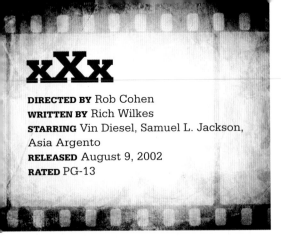

xXx

DIRECTED BY Rob Cohen
WRITTEN BY Rich Wilkes
STARRING Vin Diesel, Samuel L. Jackson, Asia Argento
RELEASED August 9, 2002
RATED PG-13

Smoking kills! Especially in the Xander Xone, named after Mister Too-Cool-For-School Xander Cage (Vin Diesel), an extreme sports athlete with a hatred of authority and cigarettes.

He's always telling people not to smoke in *xXx*, even the bad guys. When one baddie doesn't heed his advice early on, he pays the price. Xander ends up with a heat-seeking rocket launcher, which he uses to lock onto the heat from the baddies' cigarette and blows the euro trash criminal sky-high. Good thing that rocket didn't, you know, lock onto body heat instead of the tiny bit of heat from that cigarette, or Xander might've blown himself up instead. *xXx* may not be a textbook classic film, but it is an over-the-top, awesome cheesy mess that every action fan needs to see.

In a lot of ways, Xander Cage is a classic representation of the anti-hero. He doesn't actively seek out heroism, but he won't stand for injustice, either. All in all, he's actually a pretty nice guy, always trying to help people stay healthy and saving anyone who needs saving, whether he knows them or not. Plus he's active in politics, which he shows by stealing a California representative's Corvette and

VIN DIESEL

A NEW BREED OF SECRET AGENT

FROM THE DIRECTOR AND PRODUCER OF
THE FAST AND THE FURIOUS

xXx

COMING 2002

sony.com/TripleX

The outrageous action and stunts are as triple X-treme as the title.
Columbia/Revolution Studios/The Kobal Collection/Bob Marshak

XANDER CAGE:

"I live for this shit."

driving it off a 730-foot bridge while he parachutes to safety. He technically breaks the law by doing this, but Xander only wants to make a political statement. "More or less, don't be a dick, Dick!" It's nice when young people get involved in the government.

National security agent, Augustus (Samuel L. Jackson), catches wind of Xander's car-stealing shenanigans and offers him immunity from his crimes if he will go undercover to gather information on a terrorist group known as Anarchy 99. This group hates all government systems and wants to destroy them by releasing a deadly chemical weapon into the air of major cities.

Overall, *xXx* is a crazy, borderline self-aware film. Knowing that it was supposed to be an action movie, it feels like the creators decided to have fun with it by adding in every outrageous, completely unrealistic stunt they could think of, and adding in odd moments of tongue-in-cheek humor, like Xander's aforementioned hatred of smoking, or him not knowing how to turn off the safety on his gun. The action is fast paced and as triple X-treme as the title, with several sequences more outlandish than the finales of other, lesser action movies.

The Lord of the Rings Trilogy

DIRECTED BY Peter Jackson
WRITTEN BY Peter Jackson (screenplay),
Fran Walsh (screenplay), Phillipa Boyens
(screenplay), J.R.R Tolkien (novels)
STARRING Elijah Wood, Ian McKellen, Viggo
Mortensen, Sean Astin, Orlando Bloom,
John Rhys-Davies, Dominic Managhan,
Billy Boyd, Sean Bean, Christopher Lee,
Hugo Weaving, Liv Tyler
RELEASED December 19, 2001 (The
Fellowship of the Ring)
December 18, 2002 (The Two Towers)
December 17, 2003 (The Return of the King)
RATED PG-13

All of this fighting over a big of jewelry. New Line/Saul Zaentz/Wing Nut Films/The
Kobal Collection/Pierre Vinet

The Lord of the Rings trilogy, an epic
fantasy series of the highest order, also
contains some of the largest-scale action
scenes and biggest body counts of
any films. They've received worldwide
recognition with people praising the
scenery, costumes, performances, and
pretty much everything else about the
movies. It became the highest-grossing
movie trilogy in the world and has
received endless amounts of awards. Now
that's all nice and good, but this book is
for action aficionados, people who love
to watch things explode and bad guys
get their comeuppance! So that's what
this review is going to focus on. Each film
has several fabulous battles that an action
movie freak cannot ignore.

The trilogy truly is an epic story, with
the shortest running 178 minutes long,

GANDALF:

"There is only one Lord of the Ring, only one who can bend it to his will. And he does not share power."

and each film picking up right where the previous one left off. In a nutshell, the story follows hobbit Frodo Baggins (Elijah Wood) and his crew of mostly badasses as they journey through Middle-Earth to destroy one ring that holds magical powers and an evil dark lord's life force.

The Fellowship of the Ring has two battle scenes that really stick in the audience's mind. First we have the Mines of Moria, where the fellowship faces off against a horde of goblins, a cave troll, and finally, Durin's Bane himself, The Balrog. This sequence begins with a close-quarters battle in a tomb, then moves on to a frantic run through the mines before climaxing with a showdown between Gandalf the Grey (Ian McKellen) and The Balrog.

The film's finale has the fellowship doing battle against an army of Uruk-hai, who are the kind of giant, muscle-bound monsters that normal orcs wish they could be. Their leader is an Uruk named Lurtz, who is a pumped up freak with a taste for blood. Literally. I mean, the guy's so psychotic that when Aragorn (Viggo Mortensen) stabs him in the leg, he pulls out the knife and licks the blood off. Their

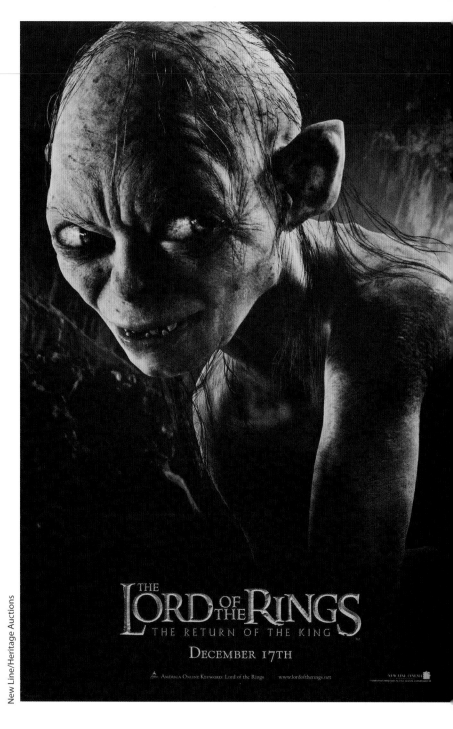

THE LORD OF THE RINGS
THE RETURN OF THE KING

DECEMBER 17TH

New Line/Heritage Auctions

what. The battle at Helm's Deep makes up a huge portion of the film and rightly so. There's so much going on, with all of the arrows flying, people getting impaled, elves getting chopped to bits, and Legolas (Orlando Bloom) sliding down a set of stairs using a shield as a skateboard, all the while shooting orcs right and left. The body count in this sequence is staggering; so high, in fact, that Legolas and Gimli (John Rhys-Davies) get a little wager going to see who can kill the most orcs.

In *The Return of the King*, the battles come a little more frequently, and the blood flows a little more readily. Early on we have the fight for Minas Tirith, where Gandalf does his badass thing and blasts some magic at some orcs to teach them a lesson about manners.

Later there's the Army of the Dead, which is exactly what it sounds like: an army of undead soldiers, cursed to hover between life and death, all ready and raring to kick some ass. We also see the introduction of the Witch-King, a villain so fierce they say no man can slay him. Spoiler alert: he didn't count on a woman trying to kill him, so when Eowyn (Miranda Otto) shows up, looking mighty pissed that the Witch-King has killed her uncle, she stabs that black-hearted bastard right in the face and sends him to bad guy heaven, also known as Hell.

The Lord of the Rings trilogy is classic in every sense of the word. Nowhere else will you find a story so epic, battle scenes so grand, or action so fantastical. Although each film may run a little long for the taste of the average action movie freak, steel yourself, and know that a film needs that much time when there's that many orcs to be killed.

one-on-one fight is a spectacular clash of finesse against brawn, and ends with Aragon impaling the beast on his sword. What does Lurtz do in his last moments? Pull Aragorn and his blade in closer, impaling himself more deeply, all so he can get one last primal roar in Aragorn's face. Gotta love a villain who stays psycho to the end!

The Two Towers, a fan favorite of the trilogy, has one of the most memorable battle scenes of any film—the clash at Helm's Deep. Since Helm's Deep is a nigh-impregnable fortress, what's any self-respecting villain to do? Throw tens of thousands of orcs at it, that's

A Better Tomorrow

DIRECTED BY John Woo
WRITTEN BY Chan Hing-Ka, Leung Suk-Wah, John Woo
STARRING Chow Yun-Fat, Ti Lung, Leslie Cheung
RELEASED February 8, 1986
RATED R

Of all of Hong Kong's action films, *A Better Tomorrow* is one of the most influential in both its native land and America. Ranking number two on the "Best 100 Chinese Motion Pictures" list, *A Better Tomorrow* is one of John Woo's most well known and culturally significant works; so significant, in fact, that it spawned two sequels and a Korean remake.

The film's plot centers around two best friends and partners in crime, Sung Tse-Ho (Ti Lung) and Mark Lee (Chow Yun-Fat), both working for the Triad as part of their business of counterfeiting US bank notes. After a deal goes awry, Ho surrenders to the police in order to save fellow Triad member Shing (Waise Lee), and as a result, he is imprisoned for three years. Meanwhile, Ho's little brother Kit (Leslie Cheung) becomes a police officer and makes it his own personal mission to bust the Triad despite his brother being a member, and his

boss telling him to knock it off.

When Ho is released from jail, he tries to start a new, crime-free life but finds his Triad ties pulling him back in. Shing, the gang's vicious new leader, pressures Ho into returning by nearly murdering his brother and then dealing Mark a savage beating. Finally, Ho realizes that peace isn't possible and goes on a quest for vengeance against Shing.

It's not just the action that makes *A Better Tomorrow* brilliant; it's how every element of the film blends together. The engaging story and meaningful character arcs pull the viewer in, then the powerful score and fantastic action scenes wow them. Unlike many other flicks in the genre, the action in *A Better Tomorrow* is used as a tool to advance the story and inter-character relationships rather than mindless booms and bangs for spectacle's sake.

Those looking for a film with a little more meat on its bones should turn to *A Better Tomorrow,* as its story of brotherly love is touching, and its action is tough enough for even the most diehard of action movie freaks to approve of.

KEN:
"If you live by principles, you have nothing to fear. Be strong."

Nothing like a smoke after some heavy bloodshed.
Cinema City Film Production/The Kobal Collection

Chow Yun-Fat is one Hard-Boiled badass. Milestone/The Kobal Collection

CHOW YUN-FAT

If an action freak has seen some of John Woo's most popular films, chances are they've seen a handsome guy wearing sunglasses, toting two guns on his hips as he chews on a toothpick, and that guy would be Hong Kong action star Chow Yun-Fat. His boyish good looks give him a face people trust instantly, and his athletic build lets him pull off insane action maneuvers, two qualities that make for an excellent hero or villain and earned him the nickname "Babyface Killer."

The Long Kiss Goodnight

DIRECTED BY Renny Harlin
WRITTEN BY Shane Black
STARRING Geena Davis, Samuel L. Jackson, Yvonne Zima
RELEASED October 11, 1996
RATED R

Oh the weather outside is frightful … and so is Samantha Caine. Or Charly Baltimore … or whatever she fancies her name to be at the time because she can do whatever the hell she wants.

Geena Davis is Samantha Caine/Charly Baltimore in *The Long Kiss Goodnight*. Originally a trained assassin, Samantha's now suffering from amnesia and doesn't remember anything from her days as a pro ass-kicker. She leads a pretty normal life as a mother and a schoolteacher, but can't help being curious about her past, enlisting the help of Mitch Henessey (Samuel L. Jackson), a crappy local detective. Eventually he stumbles into some legitimate information and the two pair up to get to the bottom of things, finding out about Samantha's sordid past and a terrorist group's plot to destroy downtown Niagara Falls, New York. The only question that remains is whether Samantha's assassin skills will resurface in time to try to stop the terrorists. (Hint: they do.)

Much of what's enjoyable about *The Long Kiss Goodnight* are the two leads, whose characters not only play to their strengths as individuals, but create a strong team between them. The rest of the film holds up well, with strong writing from legendary action writer Shane Black, plenty of car chases, and more than a few shootouts. There's also some requisite '90s extreme sporting when Samantha dons ice skates to catch up to a fleeing car.

The Long Kiss Goodnight is equipped with all the traditional Christmas activities: caroling with a gun stuck to your head, going

to church and having your kid kidnapped, going to visit your family and realizing that they are actually targets that you were once sent to kill … you know, all the usual, good stuff. Can you imagine how that Christmas went? "Happy holidays, kids! Your mom is a trained assassin and can snap a guy's neck with one hand while baking a pie with the other." Their dad might want to tell Santa to keep away from this household, or he might find a .45 caliber at the end of that chimney.

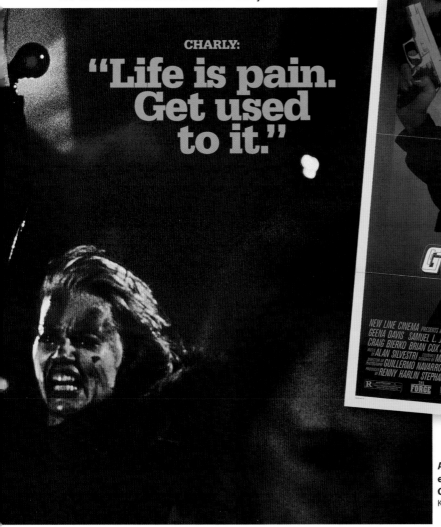

CHARLY:
"Life is pain. Get used to it."

Eight years ago she lost her memory. Now, a detective must help her remember the past before it buries them both.

THE LONG KISS GOODNIGHT
A RENNY HARLIN FILM

What's forgotten is not always gone.

As mild-mannered teacher Samantha Caine unravels her past, she morphs back into who she really is: Charly Baltimore, an assassin for the CIA. New Line/The Kobal Collection

Face/Off

DIRECTED BY John Woo
WRITTEN BY Mike Werb, Michael Colleary
STARRING John Travolta, Nicolas Cage, Joan Allen
RELEASED June 27, 1997
RELEASED R

There are quite a few times when a viewer has to utilize some suspension of disbelief in order to enjoy an action film. The audience knows a person isn't likely to survive a point-blank explosion simply by jumping away at the last moment, but they let it slide in an action movie because it's for entertainment. John Woo's *Face/Off* requires more of a suspension of disbelief than the Tooth Fairy, Santa Claus, and Tim Allen combined because of its storyline; it's like an hour-and-a-half-long sequence of people jumping away from the explosion at the last second.

FBI agent Archer (John Travolta) has been chasing terrorist Castor Troy (Nicholas Cage) for years, partly because it's his job, and partly because Troy killed Archer's son when trying to kill

CASTOR TROY:
"I'm about to unleash the biblical plague 'Hell'-A. deserves."

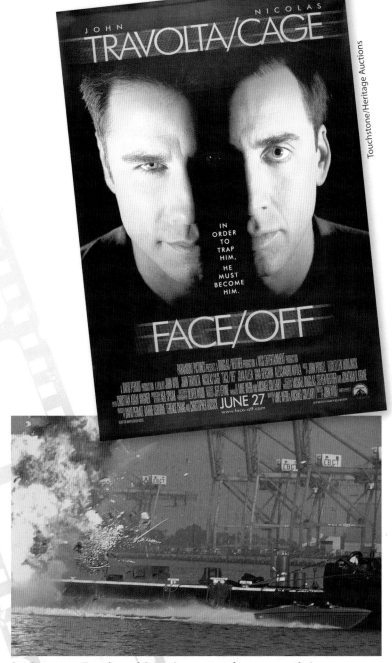

JOHN **NICOLAS**
TRAVOLTA/CAGE

IN
ORDER
TO
TRAP
HIM,
HE
MUST
BECOME
HIM.

FACE/OFF

JUNE 27
www.face-off.com

him. Eventually, Archer nabs his man and leaves him coma-stricken. When evidence arises that Troy planted a huge bomb somewhere, the FBI has to rely on unconventional means to take care of it.

Logically, the first thing the FBI suggests is an experimental procedure in which Archer undergoes a "face plant," swapping Troy's face onto his, which would totally work in real life. While Archer is undercover as Troy, the real Troy wakes up and swipes Archer's face, then Troy-Archer kills everyone who knows that Archer-Troy is actually the real Archer, and Troy-Archer goes around living Archer's life and behaving weirdly towards his teenaged daughter. Eventually Archer-Troy realizes that the only way he's getting his face back is with a face off.

The premise is absolutely ridiculous but it does allow for some great performances from the two leads. Watching Cage and Travolta transform into one another's character is fascinating; at one point, Cage is pretending to be Travolta pretending to be Cage. Viewers will struggle to remember whether Archer-Troy is really Archer, or Troy, and who's on second.

Face/Off holds a great variety of action. There's a prison fight and a shoot out between the FBI and Archer-Troy. The film breezes over the fact that Archer probably killed several of his FBI friends during that, but oh well, most of those guys were probably douches around the office. There's also a ruthless fight between Archer and Troy in the end that starts in a church, moves to a speedboat, and then crashes back on land, with each little moment containing the type of hyper-dramatic flourishes you'd expect with action expert John Woo directing.

Previous page: Travolta and Cage give great performances as their own characters and each other's. Above: The grand finale is filled with dramatic flourishes action lovers expect from director John Woo. Paramount/Touchstone/Heritage Auctions

Silverado

DIRECTED BY Lawrence Kasdan
WRITTEN BY Lawrence Kasdan, Mark Kasdan
STARRING Kevin Kline, Scott Glenn, Kevin Costner, Danny Glover
RELEASED July 10, 1985
RATED PG-13

There's a group of hat-shooting gunslingers stirring up a major stink in the classic action/western *Silverado*. In the film, a group of four men come together mostly by chance in the small town of Silverado. On the way to break his brother, Jake (Kevin Costner), out of jail, Emmett (Scott Glen) encounters Paden (Kevin Kline) in the desert, robbed and left to die. He gives him a little water and helps him reach Silverado out of the goodness of his heart, and while in town, they next come across Mal (Danny Glover), who is being forced to leave because he's black.

After a jail break-out and a high-noon shootout, the foursome bond together and decide to take down the local corrupt ranchers, a group of no-good, yeller sonsabitches who've been running around shooting people like they was going out of season.

Silverado is one of the more action-packed westerns. The first scene doesn't even have a single word of spoken dialogue before the bullets start flying. The rest of the film matches that level of intensity, with some of the best trick gunshots you'll see this side of Revolver Ocelot, and character-driven action scenes that really bring weight to each bullet. Unlike many action movies, *Silverado* works to get the audience invested in the characters, and with such a great cast portraying them, viewers will find themselves gripping the edge of their seat in the hopes that each gunshot won't spell the end for one of our heroes.

In addition to the lead actors, *Silverado* has a wonderful cast of supporting actors, including John Cleese and an insanely young Jeff Goldblum, who portray the corrupt Sheriff Langston and Slick, respectively, with each bringing their usual charm and grace to the parts. So saddle up for a fun and rocky adventure with *Silverado*.

Glover, Costner, Glenn, and Kline saddle up to take down some corrupt ranchers. Columbia/Heritage Auctions

COBB:
"We're gonna give you a fair trial, followed by a first class hanging."

Glover's Mal is not going to be kicked out of town without a fight.
Columbia/Heritage Auctions

I'm no doctor, but this man seems to have a case of the being dead. Columbia/Heritage Auctions

The Expendables

DIRECTED BY Sylvester Stallone
WRITTEN BY Dave Callaham (screenplay/story), Sylvester Stallone (screenplay)
STARRING Sylvester Stallone, Jason Statham, Jet Li, Dolph Lundgren, Terry Crews, Steve Austin, Eric Roberts, Randy Couture, Bruce Willis (!) and Arnold Schwarzenegger (!!!)
RELEASED August 13, 2010
RATED R

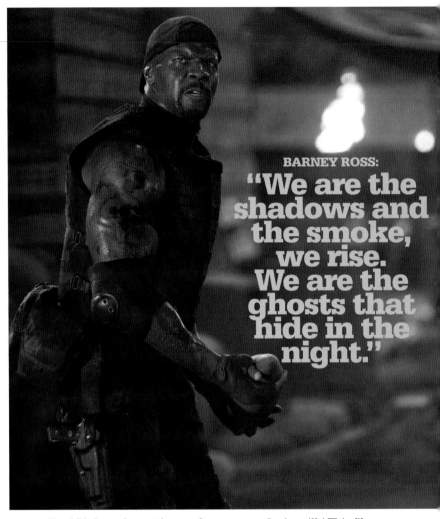

BARNEY ROSS:
"We are the shadows and the smoke, we rise. We are the ghosts that hide in the night."

The Expendables is every action movie freak's dream come true! I love it so much I want to marry it and have little expendable babies! This film brings together almost every single action legend, new and old school, into one film for a testosterone-filled blood bath. Granted, the plot and the acting certainly are not award winning, but the action and the cast are!

The film centers on a team of extremely talented mercenaries for hire who specialize in "good guy" mercenary work like recovering hostages or insane rescue missions. Led by Barney Ross (Sylvester Stallone), the Expendables are hired to go into the island of Vilena to overthrow a vicious dictator, General Garza (David Zayas). As they investigate the evil tyrant, they find that he's being backed by an extra evil man, ex-CIA agent, James Munroe (Eric Roberts), and company. The Expendables have their work cut out for them but they go in guns a blazin' and bombs a flyin'. Let the shit storm commence!

The action in *The Expendables* is astounding! It's brutal, creative, and stays crunchy in milk! This film is meant to be an action orgy and it delivers. A LOT of imagination, planning, and talented stunt performers came together to create so many different ways to kill and explode the bad guys. And with so many different action legends in the film, it'd be a shame not to highlight an awesome moment from each of them.

Barney Ross (Sylvester Stallone): Some soldiers are torturing the general's daughter (Gisele Itie), who happens to be the girl all the Expendables are trying to rescue. Big mistake, fellas! Ross doesn't care for their un-gentlemanly conduct, and decides to

Couture as Toll Road puts his professional wrestling skills to good use. Milennium Films/The Kobal Collection

Hale Caesar and Barney Ross watch the result of their handiwork. Milennium Films/The Kobal Collection

Lundgren as Gunnar Jensen. Milennium Films

teach them some manners by slicing clean through one bad guy's hand and then spinning around and completely decapitating the other guy. He finishes the one-handed clapper by stabbing him in the throat and twisting the knife like a doorknob.

Hale Caesar (Terry Crews): Picture this: You hear insanely loud gun shots, louder than anything you've ever heard. What is it? You look down a hallway and see henchmen getting blown to pieces as they're trying to run away. Then you see Caesar walk into view with a massive machine gun annihilating every baddie in his path! Uh-oh. Maybe it's time to clock out early and RUN!

Toll Road (Randy Couture): Wrestler vs. Wrestler! Road caught up to Paine (Steve Austin) and the two go at it, really showing off their wrestling skills. After body slamming each other for awhile, Road pushes Paine into a flaming river of gasoline. He goes up in flames right as Road delivers one final blow by jumping in the air and punching a flaming Paine in the face.

Yin Yang (Jet Li): Big baddie's second-hand man (Gary Daniels) is getting tag teamed by Yang and Christmas. After taking turns punching and kicking the guy, Christmas holds the guy with his head pulled back while Yang comes down with a savage kick, breaking the dude's neck and making the audience cringe.

Lee Christmas (Jason Statham): Christmas pops his head out of the nose of an airplane while Ross is flying it toward a dock chock full of enemy soldiers. He then unloads the machine gun onto the soldiers while Ross dumps fuel on them. Lee then fires a flare at the baddies,

setting off a huge explosion along the dock and killing nearly every one of them.

Gunnar Jensen (Dolph Lundgren): Two words: "Warning shot!"

Action Movie Freak's Dream Moment: How about the scene with Sylvester Stallone, Bruce Willis, and Arnold Freaking Schwarzenegger?!? If that doesn't get your pants on fire, then I don't know what will!

Li as Yin Yang (top photo) and Statham as Lee Christmas (above). These two team up to deliver a deadly Christmas present to a bad guy. Milennium Films/ The Kobal Collection Milennium Films/The Kobal Collection

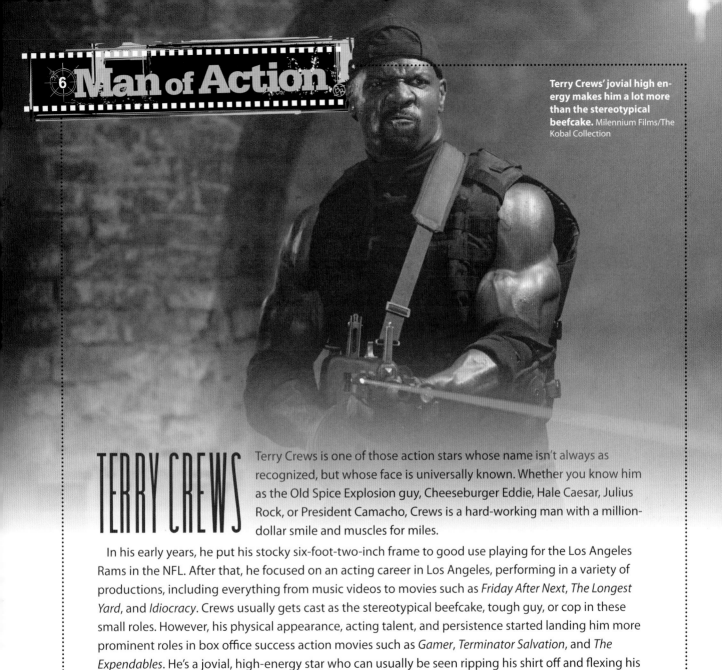

Terry Crews' jovial high energy makes him a lot more than the stereotypical beefcake. Milennium Films/The Kobal Collection

TERRY CREWS

Terry Crews is one of those action stars whose name isn't always as recognized, but whose face is universally known. Whether you know him as the Old Spice Explosion guy, Cheeseburger Eddie, Hale Caesar, Julius Rock, or President Camacho, Crews is a hard-working man with a million-dollar smile and muscles for miles.

In his early years, he put his stocky six-foot-two-inch frame to good use playing for the Los Angeles Rams in the NFL. After that, he focused on an acting career in Los Angeles, performing in a variety of productions, including everything from music videos to movies such as *Friday After Next*, *The Longest Yard*, and *Idiocracy*. Crews usually gets cast as the stereotypical beefcake, tough guy, or cop in these small roles. However, his physical appearance, acting talent, and persistence started landing him more prominent roles in box office success action movies such as *Gamer*, *Terminator Salvation*, and *The Expendables*. He's a jovial, high-energy star who can usually be seen ripping his shirt off and flexing his muscles for his audience.

Lone Wolf McQuade

DIRECTED BY Steve Carver
WRITTEN BY B.J. Nelson (screenplay/
story), H. Kaye Dyal (story)
STARRING Chuck Norris, David Carradine,
Barbara Carrera
RELEASED April 15, 1983
RATED R

**Chuck Norris doing what he does best:
Imprinting his foot print on a bad guy's
face.** Orion/The Kobal Collection

RAWLEY WILKES:

"The boys are just having a little fun.

J.J. McQuade:

You wanna join the fun?"

It's a scientific fact that the power of Chuck Norris is like no other. After all, we're talking about a man who doesn't have a chin behind his beard, he has another fist. Now, imagine if you will, the power of Chuck and beer. He'd be able to do anything! He could even magically drive his truck out of a hole after being buried alive. Sound silly? Well it's not! Chuck Norris does exactly that in *Lone Wolf McQuade*, because he is Chuck Norris and not even dirt can keep him down!

Mr. Norris portrays the titular character, J. J. McQuade, a Texas ranger with a beard as scarlet and mighty as a redwood tree. He's a quiet man with a dark past who loves his pet wolf, and prefers to work alone (don't they all?).

The plot of *Lone Wolf McQuade* is that McQuade and his greenhorn partner seek out Rawley Wilkes (David Carradine) and his evil dwarf sidekick, both of whom have been hijacking army convoys and stealing the weapons for Wilkes' illegal underground weapons trade.

With two martial arts powerhouses like David Carradine and Chuck Norris in the film, the audience would expect to see some serious fisticuffs, and *LWM* doesn't disappoint. The two juggernauts clash repeatedly, culminating in a climactic brawl so intense that both Norris and Carradine refused to use stunt doubles for it because they wanted every moment to be that much grittier and real.

On a side note, it seems like the police chief of every "Badass Who Prefers to Work Alone" is always out to get them since they keep sticking them with partners despite the fact that the cardinal trait of all of these guys is that they prefer to work alone. Maybe the police chiefs are trying to act as counselors and warm up these guys' cold hearts with a little human interaction, in which case I say, "Screw that!"

Anyway, this film has everything: tons of guns, martial arts, and beer; and, for anyone interested in men, it has shirtless, muscled-up Chuck Norris! Norris himself took such a shine to the character of Lone Wolf McQuade that one of his other, most famous characters, (Walker, Texas Ranger,) is based on him. So if you're a fan of Chuck Norris, beer, roundhouse kicks, and/or David Carradine, *Lone Wolf McQuade* is the film for you.

"Before the Boogie Man goes to sleep, he checks his closet for Chuck Norris."

Mr. Norris has become such a legend, there are an infinite amount of "facts" centered on how tough and awesome he and his beard are, and the aforementioned one is reportedly his favorite.

The world of action movies would be a different place without the Chuck and his films. Before Norris, a roundhouse kick was just a kick, nothing to get too excited about. But now, if a person says, "roundhouse kick," the biggest and baddest villains will run away with nightmares of Norris' footprints imprinted on their faces.

Outside of cinema, Norris has racked up a list of achievements a mile long. He became the Professional World Middleweight Karate Champion six times before retiring in 1974. He holds an eighth-degree black belt in Tae Kwan Do (and was the first person from the West to earn one), a 10th degree black belt in Tang Soo Do, and a black belt in Brazilian Jiu Jitsu. That's a lot of belts that basically mean don't provoke this man lest you be ripped apart.

He also has written several books, created his own form of martial arts, and opened several martial arts schools. One of his many adventures allowed him to cross paths with another legend, Bruce Lee. Norris acted as Lee's enemy in *The Way of the Dragon*, a film that ends with a massive brawl between the two martial arts titans, a fight which is often

Action icons Chuck Norris and Bruce Lee square off against each other in *The Way of the Dragon*. Concord/Golden Harvest/The Kobal Collection

considered the greatest in movie history. From there, he went on to star in numerous films such as *Lone Wolf McQuade*, *Missing in Action*, and *Delta Force*, but is most recognized for his work on television show *Walker, Texas Ranger*, where he spends 203 episodes roundhouse kicking Texas into shape. Lastly, in 2012, he graced the silver screen again amidst a sea of other action legends in *The Expendables 2*.

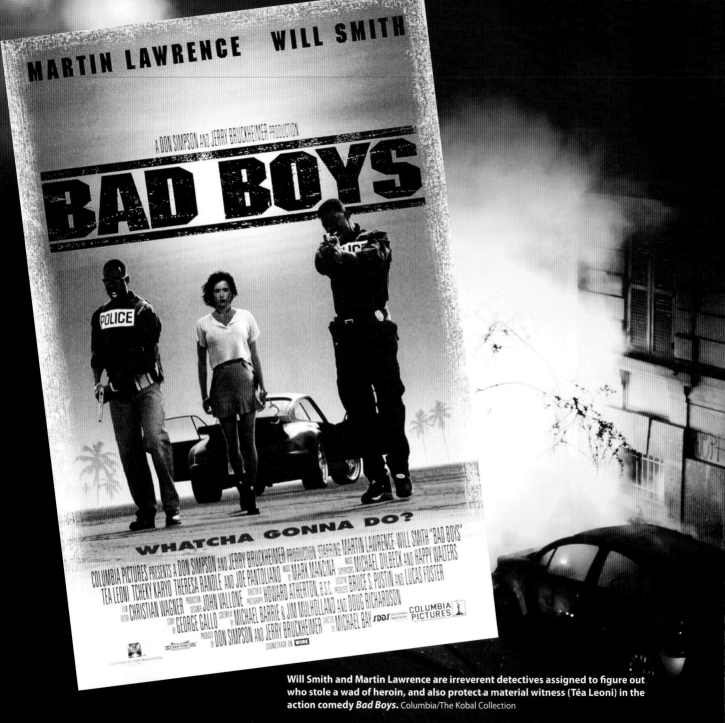

Will Smith and Martin Lawrence are irreverent detectives assigned to figure out who stole a wad of heroin, and also protect a material witness (Téa Leoni) in the action comedy *Bad Boys*. Columbia/The Kobal Collection

Buddy Cop Films

The foundation to the adult Happy Meal/action genre has been created with the bun and hamburger patty/classic action films. Now, it's time to make the foundation stronger by adding a second patty: buddy cop films.

In the buddy cop subgenre, two officers of the law get paired together to deal with a common foe. The two leads are generally cops, and they're almost never buddies at the start of the flick, thanks to their differences in culture, morals, or levels of sanity. For example, there might be a buddy cop film where one's a police officer called The Butcher, because of his brutal police methods and love of ham, and the other is an Orthodox Jew, who doesn't eat ham. Or maybe one's a person and the other's a dog. Or maybe one is Stallone and the other is that really old lady from Golden Girls.

With a long pedigree of heroic duos that can be traced back to Holmes and Watson, the original buddy cops, this genre of films tends to be more focused on inter-character chemistry than it is on big explosions or drawn-out fistfights. Despite this lower level of action, these flicks always keep the energy high, and generally that's becau they fill in the gaps with some extra dos of comedy.

A single-patty hamburger is nice and tasty, but making it a double is just good sense. After all, why only have one, when you can have two? It's double the value and the taste. So when it comes to action films, why have one action hero when there can be two? Action fans'll get double the snarky one-liners, doub the quips, and double the excitement. So when action movie freaks feel like "making it a double," they should order up one of the following films.

Kurt Russell and Sylvester Stallone are—what else?—mismatched police partners in *Tango & Cash*. Warner Bros./ Heritage Auctions

Lethal Weapon

DIRECTED BY Richard Donner
WRITTEN BY Shane Black
STARRING Mel Gibson, Danny Glover, Gary Busey, Mitchell Ryan, Tom Atkins
RELEASED March 6, 1987
RATED R

Lethal Weapon Series

Many films involve a story about cops busting drug dealers, but add a title like *Lethal Weapon,* a kickass team of leads like Mel Gibson and Danny Glover as Martin "That Guy's A Loose Cannon" Riggs and Roger "I'm Getting Too Old For This Shit" Murtaugh, respectively, and you've got yourself a recipe for a must watch '80s movie, and a perfect example of the buddy cop genre.

Now, many believe the first two *Lethal Weapon* films are the best, which is why they've been highlighted below. However, a true action movie freak should watch all of the *Lethal Weapons,* as each one offers something a little different, like the addition of Renee Russo in the third, and Jet Li and Chris Rock in the fourth.

Martin Riggs is a young police officer on the brink of suicide and/or a mental breakdown since his wife was killed in a car accident. Roger Murtaugh is a straight-laced police officer just celebrating his 50th birthday with his lovely family. These two are forced to become partners despite their differences and go out to bust some drug-dealing baddies.

This is where it all started. *Lethal Weapon* was such a hit, three sequels followed. It took No. 24 in *Entertainment Weekly's* greatest action movies of all time list and served as an inspiration for many of the other buddy cop films listed in this book.

The last third of this film contains an onslaught of excellent action sequences, like a car chase on the L.A. freeway, explosions, and a knockdown, drag-out fist fight on Murtaugh's front lawn between Riggs and Joshua (Gary Busey). Plus Mel Gibson is super ripped and not afraid to show it and his character is off-the-wall insane … must've been tough for Mel to pull that off.

ROGER MURTAUGH:
"Have you ever met anybody you didn't kill?"

This is the film that puts every element of a buddy cop film together perfectly: the two cops that are as dissimilar as peanut butter and jelly, but taste just as good together, the blend of comedy and action, and the sweet-ass saxophone music. All of these come together to show why *Lethal Weapon* is the quintessential buddy cop film.

There are almost as many verbal explosions between straight-laced Murtaugh and crazy-ass Riggs as actual ones. Warner Bros./The Kobal Collection

MARTIN RIGGS:

"Well, I haven't killed you yet."

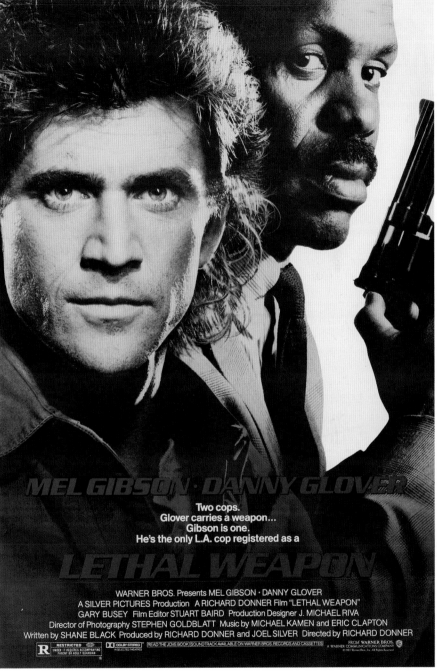

MEL GIBSON · DANNY GLOVER

Two cops.
Glover carries a weapon...
Gibson is one.
He's the only L.A. cop registered as a

LETHAL WEAPON

WARNER BROS. Presents MEL GIBSON · DANNY GLOVER
A SILVER PICTURES Production   A RICHARD DONNER Film "LETHAL WEAPON"
GARY BUSEY Film Editor STUART BAIRD Production Designer J. MICHAEL RIVA
Director of Photography STEPHEN GOLDBLATT Music by MICHAEL KAMEN and ERIC CLAPTON
Written by SHANE BLACK Produced by RICHARD DONNER and JOEL SILVER Directed by RICHARD DONNER

Warner Bros./Heritage Auctions

Lethal Weapon 2

DIRECTED BY Richard Donner
WRITTEN BY Jeffrey Boam (screenplay), Shane Black (story/characters), Shane Murphy (story)
STARRING Mel Gibson, Danny Glover, Joe Pesci
RELEASED July 7, 1989
RATED R

One of the many fantastic things about *Lethal Weapon 2* is that it opens in the middle of a car chase scene. Not just a short, half-assed chase scene, either. It's eight minutes of high-speed racing with cars crashing, metal twisting, and gas tanks exploding. Now that's how you open an action movie! *Lethal Weapon 2* cuts the crap and gets right into the good stuff.

After the great opening scene, Martin Riggs (Mel Gibson) and Roger Murtaugh (Danny Glover) are assigned to protect a witness, Leo Getz (Joe Pesci), so that they don't get involved in a separate high-profile case relating to the opening car chase. Well, it just so happens that Leo is connected to that other high-profile case, sending Murtaugh and Riggs spiraling into the middle of a drug smuggling operation once again.

Lethal Weapon is a great classic film, but *Lethal Weapon 2* has the freedom to get even crazier with the action. Between the toilet bombs, nail guns, and Riggs' nutso behavior, the audience never knows what's going to happen. Riggs is

particularly unhinged in this one. He's like a trained attack dog: calm and collected while the hot dog is on his nose, but as soon as he's given the word, he tears it to pieces. The only problem is that Riggs is the only one giving Riggs the word, so, like a poorly trained attack dog, sometimes he just goes nuts for no reason at all.

Lethal Weapon 2 is also a useful tool for teaching what not to do in particular situations. For instance, if you ever go in for a meeting with a bad guy, look around and make sure you're not standing on plastic. If you are, ask to go to the bathroom and then pop the window out of the hinges to escape because your chances of *walking* out of that meeting are not good. Also, diplomatic immunity only goes so far. Oh and don't ever sleep with Riggs, as his penis seems to have some kind of curse on it seeing as how every woman he's slept with so far has died.

The *Lethal Weapon* series is, at its core, about Riggs and Murtaugh; about Gibson and Glover. The dynamic between these two actors is fantastic and that interpersonal energy carries onto the big screen and lights it up like the blaze of a thousand sticks of dynamite.

Martin Riggs doing what he does best: acting crazy and reckless.
Warner Bros./The Kobal Collection

LEO GETZ: "Oh I get it. Bad cop, good cop."

ROGER MURTAUGH: "Shut up."

LEO GETZ: "Oh okay, bad cop, bad cop."

63

Rush Hour
1 and 2

PART 1: DIRECTED BY Brett Ratner
WRITTEN BY Ross LaManna (story),
Jim Kouf (screenplay), Ross LaManna
(screenplay)
STARRING Jackie Chan, Chris Tucker,
Ken Leung
RELEASED September 18, 1998
RATED PG-13

....

PART 2: DIRECTED BY Brett Ratner
WRITTEN BY Ross LaManna
(characters), Jeff Nathanson
STARRING Jackie Chan, Chris Tucker,
John Lone
RELEASED August 3, 2001
RATED PG-13

Cultures and cop styles clash when Hong Kong detective Lee joins forces with cocky American officer Carter to save a kidnapped girl. New Line/The Kobal Collection

Explosive action-comedy duo Chris Tucker and Jackie Chan pair up to bust crime in the buddy cop film series *Rush Hour*, which tells the story of Los Angeles Detective James Carter (Chris Tucker) being paired with Hong Kong Detective Inspector Lee (Jackie Chan). When the 11-year-old daughter of a diplomat is kidnapped, he calls his personal pal Lee to help. However, the FBI, being the elitist club that it is, doesn't want his help, so they get the LAPD to assign their least favorite detective, Carter, to keep Lee away from the investigation. Too bad neither Lee nor Carter is content to sit back and watch everyone else do all the work, and soon the duo is embroiled in a world of Chinese gangsters and foiled hostage negotiations.

Inspector Lee is a Chinese super cop out of his element in America, and Chan plays him with his usual affability, which works well to complement Tucker's Detective Carter, who is a head-strong smartass talking his way into as many fights as he talks his way out of. Each character plays to the strengths of the actor portraying him, and the two actors have an ease of interaction that leads to them forming a memorable pair.

The sequel takes place in Hong Kong while Lee and Carter are supposed to be on vacation and instead get mixed up in a case involving the Triad. Hilarity and ass kicking ensues as they try to figure out who exactly bombed the American Consulate.

The first film outranks the rest because of its superior execution of the buddy cop concept in addition to the sheer virtue of being the original, although *Rush Hour 2* does a great job encapsulating the

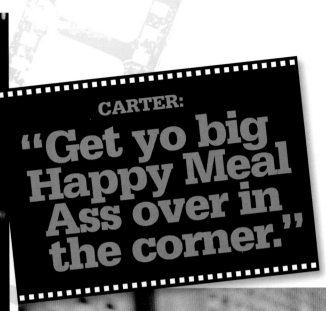

CARTER:

"Get yo big Happy Meal Ass over in the corner."

essence of the first film while still mixing it up a bit. There is a third film in the series, but the story, action scenes, and character interactions are a bit lackluster, almost as if everyone involved with the movie was tired of the franchise by the time it rolled around (the nine-year gap between the original and part three may have had something to do with that). Regardless, action movie freaks don't want to miss out on *Rush Hour 1* and *2*, two marvelous entries to the buddy cop genre.

It's more lunacy and mayhem for Carter and Lee in *Rush Hour 2*. New Line/Spyglass/The Kobal Collection/ Peter Sorel

The Rock

DIRECTED BY Michael Bay
WRITTEN BY David Weisberg (story/screenplay), Douglas Cook (story/screenplay), Mark Rosner (screenplay)
STARRING Sean Connery, Nicolas Cage, Ed Harris
RELEASED June 7, 1996
RATED R

STANLEY GOODSPEED:

"How, in the name of Zeus' butthole did you get out of your cell?"

Alcatraz Island, (otherwise known as The Rock, which is probably where they got the name for the movie), is home to a federal prison that boasts about not having a single inmate ever successfully escape during its time as a penitentiary. It being one and a half miles off the shore of San Francisco might have something to do with that.

When a group of unstable marines steal a pile of WMDs, they use Alcatraz Island as the staging ground for their shenanigans, and in the process take eighty-one tourists hostage. To help with the WMDs, the FBI turn to chemical weapon specialist Stanley Goodspeed (Nicholas Cage), and to help with the marines they call on John Mason (Sean Connery), the man who crapped on Alcatraz's record by escaping it and living to tell the tale.

Connery and Cage make a dynamite duo with the first playing the badass, as always, and the second playing a timid nerd on the brink of losing his shit, something that Cage excels at. The two display elements of an almost buddy-cop relationship, with Mason and Goodspeed huffing and puffing at each other upon their first meeting, but eventually the two bond over a cup of tea and a hail of gunfire, and they learn to appreciate each other's differences.

Though Michael Bay isn't exactly known for creating movies that are intellectually inspiring, classy, or well-thought out, the man knows how to direct an action sequence. *The Rock* is actually the exception that proves the rule, as it is one of Bay's earliest works

Helicopters zero in on Alcatraz Island. Hollywood Pictures/The Kobal Collection

and devoid of his trademark juvenile humor and sexuality, which is probably why it's his most critically acclaimed film to date. And with solid leads like Cage, Connery, Ed Harris, and great actors in secondary roles, like Tony "Don't Call Me Candyman" Todd, *The Rock* will rock you.

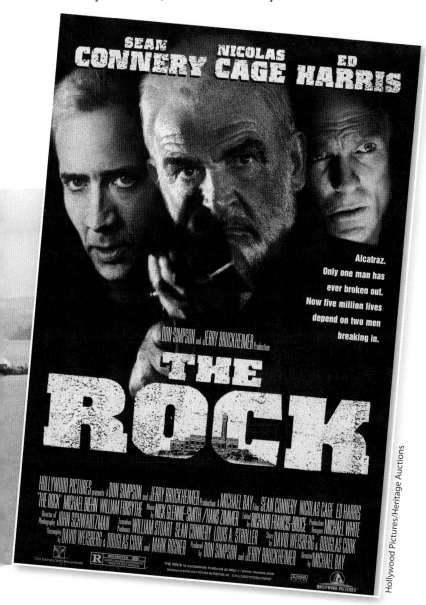

Hollywood Pictures/Heritage Auctions

Showdown in Little Tokyo

DIRECTED BY Mark L. Lester
WRITTEN BY Stephen Glantz, Caliope Brattlestreet
STARRING Dolph Lundgren, Brandon Lee, Cary-Hiroyuki Tagawa, Tia Carrere
RELEASED August 23, 1991
RATED R

Have you often had the problem of not being able to get into your car because bad guys are shooting at you? *Showdown in Little Tokyo* has just the solution! When L.A. cops Chris Kenner (Dolph Lundgren) and Johnny Murata (Brandon Lee) are being kept from their car by pesky gunfire, Kenner just tips another car up on its side and uses it as cover! So there you go, folks. All you have to do is tip a full-size car over on its side and you're golden.

For a genre not known for its excellent plot development, *Showdown in Little Tokyo* has even less story than the usual action film. Kenner and Murata are forced to become partners despite their reluctance to join forces, and are assigned to work in L.A.'s Little Tokyo section. Right off the bat they make an arrest of a guy who, as coincidence would have it, is a Yakuza clan mate of the guy who killed Kenner's father when he was a child. The Yakuza clan is in Little Tokyo and making their presence known by killing off the owner of a club and claiming it as theirs, so Kenner and Murata investigate the situation, which leads to a big showdown in the middle of Little Tokyo!

Showdown in Little Tokyo is one of those action films where the plot has to be basically overlooked, but will entertain the pants off of you with its over-the-top action and the nacho cheesefest that is the dialogue. Plus the two leads are Dolph Lundgren and Brandon Lee, son of Bruce Lee, giving it a nice boost of star power.

After the untimely death of Brandon Lee, this film has become more appreciated. It showcases Lee's martial arts skills (like father, like son) and is one for action movie freaks who are fans of Lee, Lundgren, or cheeky action with no plot.

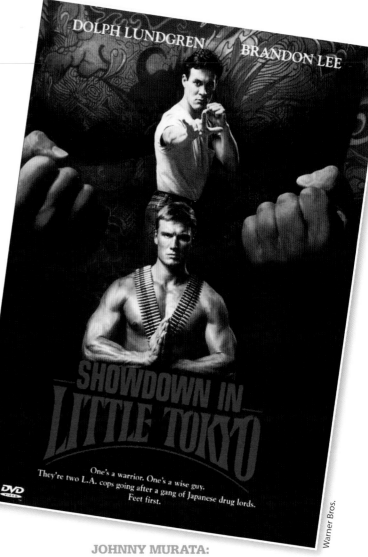

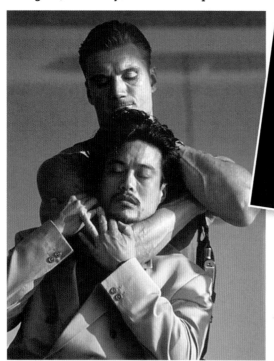

When he's not drinking tea, cop-on-the-edge Chris Kenner likes to kick a lot of Yakuza ass.
Warner Bros.

JOHNNY MURATA:

"We've got a problem here. There are more bad guys than we've got bullets."

Bad boys had better run because Marcus Burnett (Martin Lawrence) and Mike Lowery (Will Smith) are two detectives with a serious streak of bad boy-ness themselves, meaning that these detectives will use whatever force necessary to keep the streets of Miami safe.

Unlike the typical buddy cop films where two cops opposite in nature are forced to work together, Marcus and Mike have been

Bad Boys 1 and 2

PART 1: DIRECTED BY by Michael Bay
WRITTEN BY George Gallo (story), Michael Barrie (screenplay), Jim Mulholland (screenplay), Doug Richardson (screenplay)
STARRING Will Smith, Martin Lawrence, Tea Leoni
RELEASED April 7, 1995
RATED R

....

PART 2: DIRECTED BY Michael Bay
WRITTEN BY George Gallo (characters), Marianne Wibberley (story), Cormac Wibberley (story) Ron Shelton (story), Ron Shelton (screenplay), Jerry Stahl (screenplay)
STARRING Will Smith, Martin Lawrence, Gabrielle Union
RELEASED July 18, 2003
RATED R

It's more bullets and buddy-cop banter for Lawrence and Smith in *Bad Boys II*.
Columbia/The Kobal Collection/John Bramley

best friends and partners for years at the beginning of the first *Bad Boys*. This simple deviation to the established formula opens up a new dynamic between the two partners, giving them sequel-levels of trust and character interactions, often leading to crazier action sequences and more fast-paced comedy.

The Miami-Dade police department has $100 million of confiscated heroin stolen from their secure vault in *Bad Boys* (it must not be *that* secure) so Mike and Marcus step up to the plate! Internal affairs gives the department five days to recover the stolen heroin or else the narcotics division will be shut down.

Eight years after the happenings of the first film, *Bad Boys II* has detectives Marcus and Mike investigating the supercharged ecstasy that's been making its way around Miami, killing many unsuspecting club-goers and making for some rich drug dealers. At the same time, Mike has to find a way to tell Marcus he's dating his sister, and Marcus debates whether or not he wants to continue being Mike's partner.

The series is directed by Michael Bay, so, of course, the action sequences are absolutely top-notch. In *Bad Boys II*, there is a lengthy chase scene that starts with a criminal gunning down the driver of an SUV, then taking off, with Mike and Marcus in hot pursuit.

After a brief pit-stop to have a shootout with the cops, the criminals swipe another vehicle—a semi truck with a load of cars on its back—and speed down the Miami highway, releasing cars and boats onto the busy highway and causing a chain reaction of car crashes, topping it all off with an explosion!

Though the scripts for the *Bad Boys* films may often delve into misogynistic and homophobic humor, the charisma and natural comedic talents of Will Smith and Martin Lawrence help propel the films forward even when things are getting unfunny and *way* politically incorrect.

MIKE LOWREY:
"You know, you drive almost slow enough to drive Miss Daisy."

The propane tank indicates it's not a Michael Bay movie without things blowing up. Columbia/The Kobal Collection

Will Smith is so cool, he can even deliver squid-type alien babies in *Men in Black*. Columbia/ The Kobal Collection

WILL SMITH

Will Smith is one of the most bankable actors in the world, and the man's talent and sense of hard work certainly have something to do with that. In west Philadelphia, he was born and raised … before he achieved success as a hip-hop artist, success that ultimately landed him a television show based on his life, *The Fresh Prince of Bel-Air*. Smith is one of the few musicians-turned-actors who are better known as an actor, rather than a musician. Part of that may be because he's, you know, actually good, unlike some of his other contemporaries (remember Vanilla Ice's *Cool as Ice*? Didn't think so).

To an action audience, he's known for playing mostly cops or some kind of special agent, often with names that start with "J." His action credits include the *Bad Boys* series, *Independence Day*, *Men in Black* series, *Hancock*, and *I, Robot*. Smith manages to balance strength as a hero and powerful comedic timing, often livening up what might have otherwise been a dry-as-bones action movie. He's not strictly an action star, nor is he probably the first person people think of in the action genre, but nonetheless, his contributions to this genre are enormous, and he always performs with charm, style, and just a dab of "aw, hell naw!"

Hard Boiled

DIRECTED BY John Woo
WRITTEN BY John Woo (story), Barry Wong (screenplay), Gordon Chan (screenplay, uncredited)
STARRING Chow Yun-Fat, Tony Leung Chiu-Wai, Teresa Mo
RELEASED April 16, 1992 (Hong Kong)
RATED R

There's a reason the films of John Woo keep popping up in this book: the man knows how to direct an action scene! You can always count on his films to deliver great action and *Hard Boiled* is no exception.

This Hong Kong flick centers on Inspector Tequila (Chow Yun-Fat). After losing his police partner in a gun fight, Tequila makes it his mission to get revenge on the gangsters who killed him. While investigating the gang, he discovers an undercover cop, Tony (Tony Leung), has already infiltrated the group, and together they find out that the gang is housing a hidden arsenal in a nearby hospital, which leads to one hell of an ultimate showdown.

Hard Boiled opens with a legendary action scene set

ALAN:
"Pang said you don't waste bullets."

TEQUILA:
"Are you testing me?"

Inspector "Tequila" Yuen is as skilled at wielding firearms as he is a clarinet. Milestone/The Kobal Collection

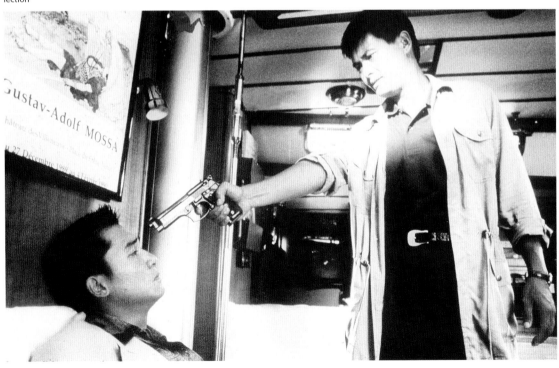

in a teahouse, of all places. When filming *Hard Boiled*, Woo discovered that the teahouse was to be torn down, and decided to do the noble thing and accelerate the process by wrecking the shit out of it with a massive shootout between the police and some gun smugglers. This scene is chock full of the kind of stylish cinematography and choreography that John Woo's films are

The general consensus is that the action in *Hard Boiled* is some of the best ever filmed. Milestone/The Kobal Collection

famous for, like a shot of Inspector Tequila sliding down a banister on his back, blasting smugglers all the way down. Then at the end, Inspector Bad Ass Tequila rolls across a kitchen table and comes up, covered in flour, pointing his gun right against the last standing bad guy's head. With a smirk, he spits out his trademark toothpick and blows a hole in the bad guy's head, leaving a spatter of brains and blood across his own face. Sweet!

The two lead characters, Tequila and Tony, have an interesting, buddy-cop-esque relationship. They're partners in that they're trying to achieve the same goal and end up working together to do it, but there's no trust between them, and they try to kill each other several times throughout the movie. They do end up saving each other as much as they try to kill each other, so it all evens out.

An action movie freak can't go wrong with *Hard Boiled*'s fascinating fight sequences, huge ass explosions, and intriguing character relationships.

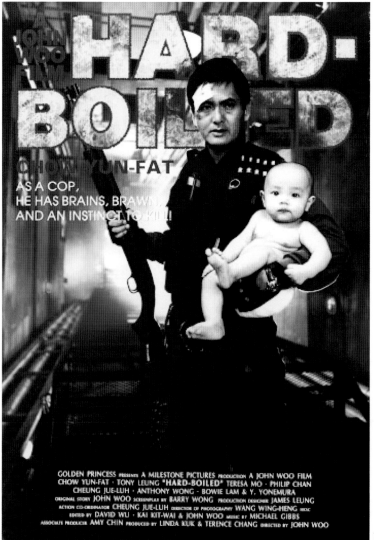

Milestone

Police Story 3: Supercop

DIRECTED BY Stanley Tony
WRITTEN BY Edward Tang (characters/story), Fibe Ma, Yee Lee Wai
STARRING Jackie Chan, Michelle Yeoh, Maggie Cheung, Yuen Wah
RELEASED July 26, 1996 (USA)
RATED R

The action in Jackie Chan's films tends to be all martial arts and amazing stunts, but *Supercop* mixes it up with America's favorite pastime: shooting guns! Sure, it's kind of weird to see Jackie Chan shooting people, but it's not long until he's back to doing what he's best at—beating people up with random household objects. Right by his side is Michelle Yeoh, who brings truth to the statement, "Girls can do anything boys can do." Yeoh performed all of her own stunts in *Supercop,* and, as any stunt performer will tell you, stunts don't always go as planned. In fact, during the credits you can see an outtake where Yeoh falls out of a moving car onto the highway. Maybe a stuntwoman would've been a good idea for that take, eh, Michelle?

Supercop is about an easygoing Hong Kong super cop, "Kevin" Chan Ka-Kui (Chan) who gets partnered up with by-the-books Interpol Inspector Jessica Yang (Yeoh), in order to catch drug lord Chaibat (Kenneth Tsang) and shut down his organization. The two have to go deep undercover and, after Chaibat orders them to help break his wife out of prison, they have to walk a fine line between keeping their cover and aiding a criminal.

One thing *Supercop* does better than oodles of other films is the development of the lead female character. Yang is smart, tough, and just antagonistic enough to her male counterpart to be funny, rather than just being a bitch for the sake of bitchiness. The character interactions are helped by the fact that Chan and Yeoh have a natural "buddy cop" vibe and both have a flair for physical finesse.

A movie that's "action with a smile," *Supercop* mixes high energy stunt work with doses of comedic misunderstandings that would fit right in on *Three's Company,* and the "odd couple" style character dynamics between the two leads are a brilliant example of what makes the buddy cop genre so watchable.

CHAN KA KUI:
"Super cops in Hong Kong are cheap and plentiful, like commodities in supermarkets."

Yeoh and Chan have a natural buddy cop vibe and show a flair for physical finesse.
Golden Harvest/The Kobal Collection

Hell on Heels

MICHELLE YEOH

Despite not having any official martial arts training, Michelle Yeoh has achieved greatness as one of the world's most well known martial arts/action stars. Yeoh is known as someone who is determined and fearless, often doing her own stunt work and earning her the nickname as Hong Kong's "Queen of Martial Arts."

Yeoh's first acting role was in a commercial with Jackie Chan. She then took the lead in *Yes, Madam* and went to co-star with Chan in *Police Story 3: Supercop*. In the end credits of the latter, there are bloopers of Yeoh performing some of the film's dangerous stunts, which speaks volumes about her talent and tenacity given the fact that Jackie Chan often insists that actresses don't do their own stunt work.

Afterward, she became well known to American audiences as the lead Bond girl in *Tomorrow Never Dies* and for her role in *Crouching Tiger, Hidden Dragon* with Chow Yun-Fat and Jet Li. Her prestigious work provides a great example that an actor doesn't have to start off with a mastery of martial arts in order to be an action star.

Tango & Cash

DIRECTED BY Andrei Konchalovsky
Albert Magnoli (uncredited replacement)
WRITTEN BY Randy Feldman
STARRING Sylvester Stallone, Kurt Russell, Jack Palance, Teri Hatcher
RELEASED Dec. 22, 1989
RATED R

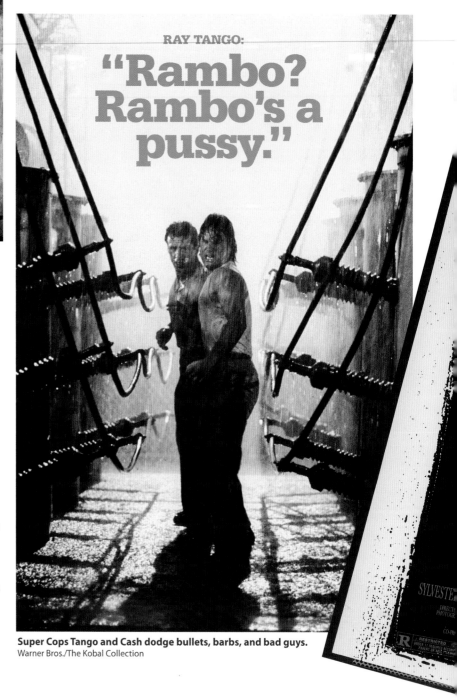

RAY TANGO:

"Rambo? Rambo's a pussy."

Super Cops Tango and Cash dodge bullets, barbs, and bad guys.
Warner Bros./The Kobal Collection

A handy metric to use when figuring out just how good a cop is at his job is to measure the number of bad guys out to get him. Having just one or two baddies dedicating all of their resources into taking a cop out is an honor; it means that he is so good that those criminals know they can't commit any crimes without drawing the attention of this master cop. Having three to five baddies on his tail means he's a freakin' badass. Ten or more upgrades a cop to super-badass. Past fifteen means he's RoboCop, and beyond fifty nets him the title of Super Cop.

In *Tango & Cash*, you've got two Super Cops, each with their own massive piles of bad guys out to take them down. Things look grim for our heroes until they team up against the seedy criminal element. Two Super Cops + a near infinite pile of disposable villains = a massive beat down the likes of which this world has never seen. Now that's the kind of math I can get behind!

Tango & Cash is a classic buddy cop movie starring action titans Sylvester

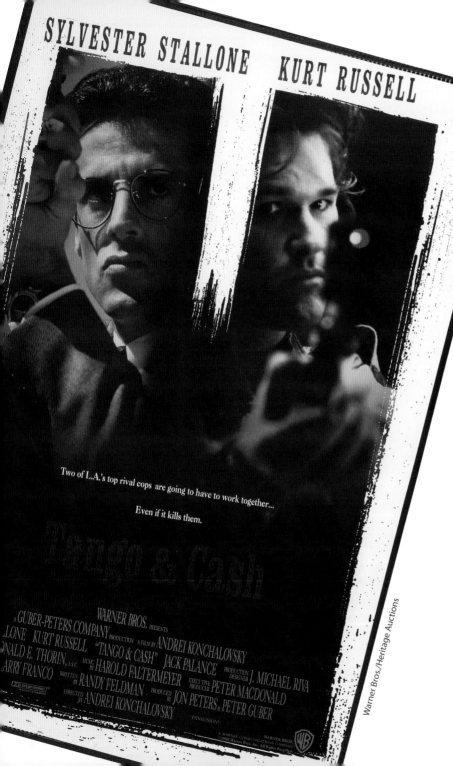

Two of L.A.'s top rival cops are going to have to work together...

Even if it kills them.

Tango & Cash

WARNER BROS. PRESENTS

A GUBER-PETERS COMPANY PRESENTS
...LONE KURT RUSSELL PRODUCTION A FILM BY ANDREI KONCHALOVSKY
...NALD E. THORIN, A.S.C. "TANGO & CASH" JACK PALANCE PRODUCTION DESIGNER J. MICHAEL RIVA
...RRY FRANCO MUSIC BY HAROLD FALTERMEYER EXECUTIVE PRODUCER PETER MACDONALD
WRITTEN BY RANDY FELDMAN PRODUCED BY JON PETERS & PETER GUBER
DIRECTED BY ANDREI KONCHALOVSKY
PANAVISION®

A WARNER COMMUNICATIONS COMPANY
©1989 Warner Bros. Inc. All Rights Res...

Stallone and Kurt Russell. Stallone gets to play the clean cut, plays-by-the-book narcotics detective Lt. Ray Tango, which is sort of a departure from the usual character Stallone plays. Russell is the loose cannon, sloppily dressed, does-what-he-needs-to-do-to-get-a-job-done-by-the-books-be-damned, Lt. Gabriel Cash. These two detectives are not only opposite in personality but are also rivals at their job, always competing to see who can get the bigger drug bust, until one day fate forces them to become partners.

The film's primary antagonist, Yves Perret (Jack Palance), is tired of having his deals busted, and conspires with a gaggle of other criminals to get Tango and Cash framed for murder, leaving the two Super Cops in prison surrounded by the thugs they've spent the last decade locking up.

Tango & Cash has the perfect trifecta: the dialogue is corny, but in a good way, the two leads are behemoths of action that audiences will instantly like, and there's enough action to pile drive viewers face first into their coffee table if they're not ready. The film has a few stunts so large-scale and dangerous that the stunt team could only do them once, and the crew had to use at least 11 cameras in order to catch everything because there was no, "Oh wait, my mom was calling. Can we do that again?" Thanks, stunt team, for putting your lives on the line to bring action movie freaks a little joy and happiness.

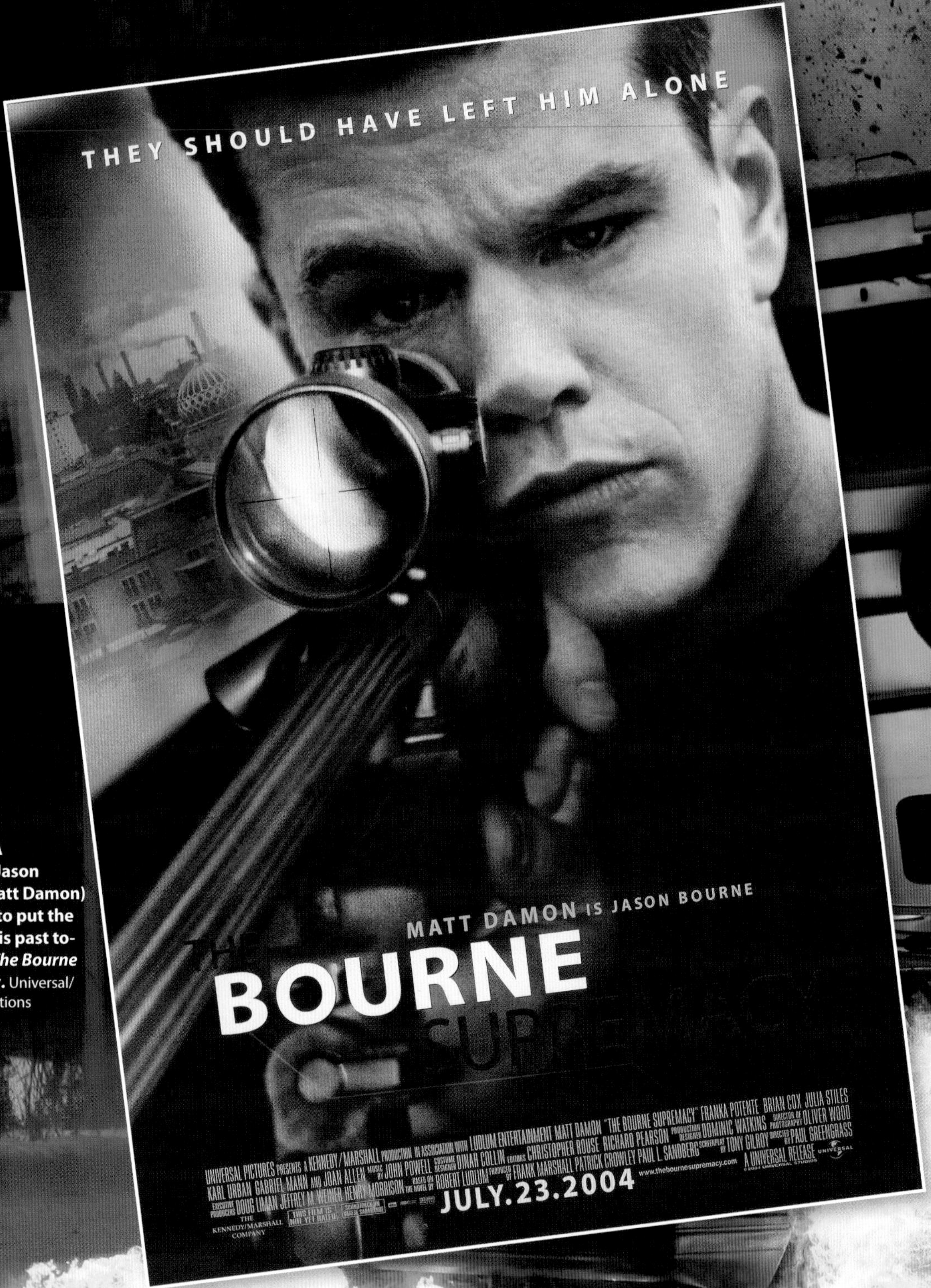

THEY SHOULD HAVE LEFT HIM ALONE

MATT DAMON IS JASON BOURNE

BOURNE
SUPREMACY

Former CIA operative Jason Bourne (Matt Damon) continues to put the pieces of his past together in *The Bourne Supremacy.* Universal/Heritage Auctions

UNIVERSAL PICTURES PRESENTS A KENNEDY/MARSHALL PRODUCTION IN ASSOCIATION WITH LUDLUM ENTERTAINMENT MATT DAMON "THE BOURNE SUPREMACY" FRANKA POTENTE BRIAN COX JULIA STILES KARL URBAN GABRIEL MANN AND JOAN ALLEN MUSIC JOHN POWELL COSTUME DINAH COLLIN EDITORS CHRISTOPHER ROUSE RICHARD PEARSON PRODUCTION DOMINIC WATKINS PHOTOGRAPHY OLIVER WOOD BASED ON ROBERT LUDLUM PRODUCED FRANK MARSHALL PATRICK CROWLEY PAUL L. SANDBERG SCREENPLAY TONY GILROY DIRECTED PAUL GREENGRASS EXECUTIVE DOUG LIMAN JEFFREY M. WEINER HENRY MORRISON www.thebournesupremacy.com A UNIVERSAL RELEASE

JULY.23.2004

THE KENNEDY/MARSHALL COMPANY

BACON STRIPS

Sequels That Hit Harder and Explode Better

Now that we have our second patty on board, I'd say the beef has been pretty well taken care of in this tour of action-y deliciousness. Now it's time to start adding on some extras. What makes two big slabs of meat taste even better? Thinner, crispier slabs of meat, that's what. I'm talking about bacon, fool! Bacon adds that fatty deliciousness that really enhances the existing fatty deliciousness of the beef.

The bacon of action movies are those sequels that hit harder and explode better! They take the meat from the first film and amp it up by throwing in more tasty action, more meaningful character development, and funnier zingers, thus enhancing the overall flavor. Since the characters' personalities have already been established in the first movie, sequels can jump right into the good stuff without having to fart around with things like "establishing character" or "plot."

Now, the original film in a series is often the best, but there are a few occasions in the action genre where the sequel outdoes the original. Sometimes it's a more intricate story woven in a way to sneak into your heart and uplift your spirits. But most of the time it's just got more punching and blowing stuff up.

Just for clarity, I'm not only talking about movies that come second in a series, I'm including any sequel, remake, or reboot, as each of these kinds of films uses the source material as a reference point to give it the potential to fly even higher.

All Alice (Milla Jovovich) needs is her new superhuman strength, speed, agility - and trusty shotgun - to fight zombies and mutant monsters in *Resident Evil: Apocalypse.* Davis Films/Impact Pictures/Ralph Konow

First Blood

DIRECTED BY Ted Kotcheff
WRITTEN BY David Morrell (novel),
Michael Kozoll (screenplay), William
Sackheim (screenplay), Sylvester
Stallone (screenplay)
STARRING Sylvester Stallone, Brian
Dennehy, Richard Crenna
RELEASED October 22, 1982
RATED R

If a series of action movies were to ever outdo the original in terms of action, it'd have to be *Rambo*. *Rambo: First Blood Part II*, *Rambo III*, and *Rambo* (yes, the fourth film is just *Rambo*) are all leaps and bounds beyond the first *Rambo* film (*First Blood*), which, don't get me wrong, is good in its own way, but is a completely different movie from the rest of the series. It does form a strong foundation for the character of John Rambo (Sylvester Stallone), a shell-shocked Vietnam veteran, and explores why he is the way he is.

The *Rambo* series is one of the best action film series ever. The action in this first flick, however, is nowhere close to the action standard set by the rest. After all, the only death in *First Blood* is one guy, and even that could be deemed an accidental death. Compare this to the kill count for even *Rambo: First Blood Part II* and it just comes up short in the body bag department. Of course, be sure to give the first film a watch because that's where it all started and has inspired many other films and parodies, but the last three films are where the awesome action's at!

TRAUTMAN:
"I don't think you understand. I didn't come to rescue Rambo from you. I came here to rescue you from him."

Carolco/Tri-Star/The Kobal Collection

A sheriff's deputy gets a close look at the bottom of Rambo's boot. Carolco/Heritage Auctions

John Rambo's commanding officer, Col. Trautman (Crenna), tries to save both his friend and the sheriff's department before things spiral out of control. Carolco/Heritage Auctions

Rambo: First Blood Part II

DIRECTED BY George P. Cosmatos
WRITTEN BY David Morrell (characters), Kevin Jarre (story), Sylvester Stallone (screenplay), James Cameron (screenplay)
STARRING Sylvester Stallone, Richard Crenna, Charles Napier
RELEASED May 22, 1985
RATED R

The ass kicking increases exponentially in *Rambo: First Blood Part II*. Rambo actually kills some people ... on purpose! This time Rambo (Sylvester Stallone) is called upon to go into Vietnam to take pictures of what everyone thinks is an abandoned POW camp, given orders that he's there as a photographer only, and

Rambo was here. Tri-Star/Heritage Auctions

81

JOHN RAMBO:
"Sir, do we get to win this time?"

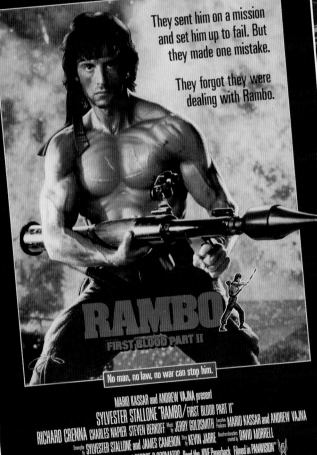

Vietnamese soldiers don't take too kindly to a local woman (Julia Nickson) who helps Rambo escape from their capture. Tri-Star/Heritage Auctions

under no circumstances should he engage the enemy. Yeah, right. Telling Rambo not to engage the enemy is like telling a fat house dog not to eat the warm turkey leg that just dropped to the floor.

Introduced in this film is Rambo's most spectacular weapon and his second best friend (next to Richard Crenna). Three words: exploding arrow heads! With these tiny explosive devices, Rambo manages to do some friggin' wide-scale damage.

In an unusual twist for the *Rambo* series, Rambo actually finds a love interest in this movie. However, before you go and try to trick someone who doesn't like action films into watching this by saying it's basically *Dirty Dancing* but with guns, you should know that she totally dies, leaving everything good and well, with Rambo blowing up bad guys by the third reel.

"Who are you?"

"Your worst nightmare."

Like a prostitute who's good at her job, *Rambo III* gives all the action the audience wants and leaves no desire unfulfilled. It also proves that just when you think there are no new ways for Rambo to stop a bad guy, he comes back with a whole new can of whoop ass.

Who does Rambo destroy this time? The Soviets! After Rambo's only friend and ally Colonel Trautman (Richard Crenna) is captured by the Soviets during a mission to supply Afghani freedom fighters with weapons, the Rambo killing machine gets activated and goes in after him, along the way enlisting the help of the obnoxious kid sidekick that was requisite in the '80s. Don't worry, though, pretty quickly that stupid kid gets booted to the curb and Rambo takes over the wheel. He is, after all, a killing machine.

The plot of *Rambo III* doesn't hold up well over time, seeing as how Rambo and his crew were helping Afghanistan escape from Soviet rule, and that a lot of the guys they were helping probably ended up becoming Al Qaeda.

After three films, Colonel Trautman's job has become really

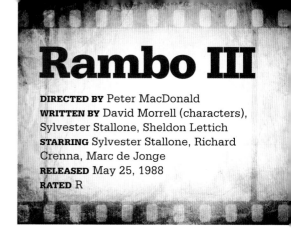

Rambo III

DIRECTED BY Peter MacDonald
WRITTEN BY David Morrell (characters), Sylvester Stallone, Sheldon Lettich
STARRING Sylvester Stallone, Richard Crenna, Marc de Jonge
RELEASED May 25, 1988
RATED R

evident: he's Rambo's hype man! He exists solely to hype Rambo's badass-itude to the other characters and the audience. Hell, most of Trautman's lines consist of things like, "You don't have to hunt Rambo, he'll hunt you." Or "I hope you brought a big enough supply … of body bags." And when a villain asks Trautman, "Who do you think this man [Rambo] is? God?" he simply replies, "No. God would have mercy. He [Rambo] won't …."

There are hardly any words that can describe the amount of action in this film. Nonstop, realistic, scary, overwhelming, and magnificent are just a few things someone could say about this movie. I have

Lionsgate

never in my life seen a movie as real and uncut as this one, and I have seen a lot of action flicks. Definitely not a movie for those who are weak of the stomach or the heart, *Rambo (IV)* is a movie for people who love war films and can take a ton of blood and guts being spewed everywhere.

Twenty years after the events of *Rambo III,* Rambo is living a quiet little life in Thailand near the Burmese border. Sarah (Julie Benz) convinces him to take her group

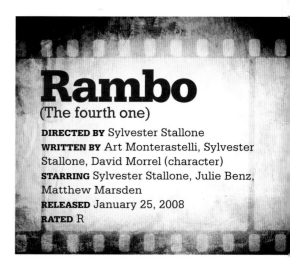

Rambo
(The fourth one)

DIRECTED BY Sylvester Stallone
WRITTEN BY Art Monterastelli, Sylvester Stallone, David Morrel (character)
STARRING Sylvester Stallone, Julie Benz, Matthew Marsden
RELEASED January 25, 2008
RATED R

of missionaries into Burma, which is embroiled in a hailstorm of political protests and war, so that they can hand out supplies. While there, the group is kidnapped by the malicious Tatmadaw soldiers who have been pillaging and burning villages all over Burma. Rambo is asked to lead a team of mercenaries to save the missionaries ... and then the bodies start cropping up.

The first scene of the film is real video of Burma in its disturbed state. The audience is treated to real footage of dead people, injuries, and the military doing not so great things, which both sets up the framework for the movie and highlights the deplorable conditions of Burma at the time.

RAMBO:
"Live for nothing. Or die for something."

The next scene (not real life footage) involves Burmese military taking citizens out into a nice little field to play a relaxing little game of fetch ... or die. The moviemakers spare you nothing; people exploding, shooting children, raping women, cutting/ blowing off arms and legs, throwing babies in fires ... this one has it all. Stallone wanted to draw a picture for everyone of the horrible situation that is happening in Burma, and I have to say, mission accomplished.

One thing about *Rambo IV* is that every single character gets involved in the action and almost every single character kills someone. Even the religious guy who claims "taking a life is never right" ends up bashing a dude's skull in. And this outing sees Rambo teamed up with a group of elite badasses, all of whom spend most of their screen time either chewing scenery with their

Bodies have a way of stacking up the further Rambo is pushed. Lionsgate

Rambo's cure for a stomachache? A knife. Lionsgate

HOW THE BODIES STACK UP IN THE RAMBO MOVIES

FIRST BLOOD:

Accidental kills by Rambo 1 (ish)

RAMBO: FIRST BLOOD PART II:

Bad guys killed by a shirt-wearing Rambo 12

Bad guys killed by shirtless Rambo 46

Total bad guys killed by Rambo 58

RAMBO III

Bad guys killed by a shirt-wearing Rambo 33

Bad guys killed by shirtless Rambo 45

Total bad guys killed by Rambo 78

RAMBO (the fourth one):

Bad guys who get their throats ripped out by Rambo 1

Bad guys killed by Rambo 83

grizzled dialogue or blasting the bad guys into tiny, bite-sized pieces.

Speaking of the baddies, few films create a picture of villains so deplorable as the Tatmadaw soldiers. Since viewers see these guys doing pretty much every horrifying, wretched thing a human being is capable of, it makes it all the more satisfying to see Rambo step in and take them down a few notches. One of the best take downs in action movies is in *Rambo*. Right as a really bad guy is undoing his belt buckle with an evil glint in his eye as he looks at Sarah, Rambo pops up behind him from out of nowhere, gets the guy in a head lock and wraps his hand around his throat. At first it's unclear what's happening, but you see the blood dripping down onto the guy's shirt and then see Rambo tear the guy's throat with his bare hands. Now that's what they call taking a "hands-on" approach!

Action movie freaks basically need balls of steel to watch this movie. It's unrelenting and action packed, with a beloved hero and super hated villains. Do you have what it takes? Of course you do; you're reading this book.

Escape from New York

DIRECTED BY John Carpenter
WRITTEN BY John Carpenter, Nick Castle
STARRING Kurt Russell, Lee Van Cleef, Ernest Borgnine
RELEASED July 10, 1981
RATED R

I guess we know what kind of snake Plissken is ... a *constrictor*. Avco Embassy/Heritage Auctions

Name: Snake Plissken.
Occupation: Badass.
Avco Embassy/Heritage Auctions

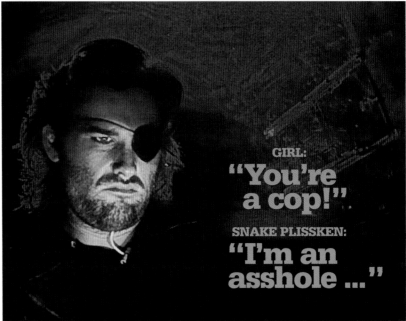

GIRL:
"You're a cop!"

SNAKE PLISSKEN:
"I'm an asshole ..."

The topic of *Escape from New York* vs. *Escape from L.A.* is a double-edged sword. The original, *Escape from New York*, by far exceeds the sequel, *Escape from L.A.,* in popularity and originality. However, the second flies higher in terms of action. So let's talk about them both!

Escape from New York introduces the audience to seasoned ex-special forces soldier, Snake Plissken (Kurt Russell), who turns to a life of crime. He's offered a full pardon for his crimes if he agrees to go into Manhattan and rescue the president, who was taken hostage by a group of inmates, within 24 hours. Snake agrees to take the mission and is injected with microscopic explosives so that if he ditches the deal and tries to run off, boom! He explodes. If he doesn't rescue the president within 24 hours, boom! He explodes. On his journey to not explode, he encounters bizarre sub-societies in the ruined wreckage of New York, including a gang of hardened criminals lead by none other than Chef himself, Isaac Hayes.

Along his way to rescue the president, Snake picks up some allies: Cabbie (Ernest Borgnine), Brain (Harry Dean Stanton), and Maggie (Adrienne Barbeau). Avco Embassy/Heritage Auctions

Snake has his charming ways of getting information from people. Avco Embassy/Heritage Auctions

Escape from L.A.

DIRECTED BY John Carpenter
WRITTEN BY John Carpenter (characters/screenplay/story), Nick Castle (characters), Debra Hill (story), Kurt Russell (story)
STARRING Kurt Russell, Steve Buscemi, Stacy Keach
RELEASED August 9, 1996
RATED R

More than fifteen years later came a sequel, *Escape from L.A.* In it, the year is 2013 and part of California has been turned into an island due to flooding. With no escape from the island, it acts as the U.S.'s prison where criminals are sent to fend for themselves. Snake, still a criminal even after what happens in the first film, departs on his journey to the island when propositioned by the President for another mission. This time, Snake will be pardoned of his crimes if he infiltrates L.A. and retrieves a device designed to shut down the world's electronics. He has 10 hours and is injected with a deadly virus so that if he doesn't succeed or tries to run, he dies. Hmm ... this sounds familiar, somehow.

The sequel had a bigger budget, allowing director John Carpenter to really go wild with it. As a result, the action is more frequent, more violent, and more awesome-er. Even so, the originality of the story is where the sequel falls flat. Amped-up action without an original story backing it up makes some people feel like the sequel is just a shallow shell of

the first. For action lovers, however, it can still be really enjoyable because there's grizzly badass Snake Plissken, with the addition of other well-loved actors such as Pam Grier, Steve Buscemi, and Bruce Campbell, who engages in an epic battle with star Kurt Russell to determine whose chin is the manliest. Ultimately, though, for many, the real driving force behind these films is Snake Plissken himself, a legendary anti-hero with a raspy voice and a knack for shooting people who get in his way. Plissken is such an influential hero, in fact, that he was the inspiration for the character of Solid Snake from the smash hit game series *Metal Gear Solid*.

In part, the lack of budget for *Escape from New York* contributes to the charm, as it's clear that everyone put in 3,459 percent extra effort to make the first film happen despite the tiny budget. The colorful characters and ever-ticking clock of *Escape from New York* keep the audience's interest high and the tension taut.

So yes, *Escape from L.A.* explodes harder than the first in terms of action, but *Escape from New York* beats the pants off it in terms of originality and development of story. Ultimately, both films are worth watching, depending on what mood the action freak is in.

SNAKE PLISSKEN:

"Your rules are really beginning to annoy me."

In total, there are currently five *Fast and Furious* films, and one more on the way, all with equally confusing names. The fifth installment outdoes the previous films in every way possible. It made more money, audiences enjoyed it more, and critics praised it more. *Fast Five* understands everything that made the previous movies enjoyable and incorporates those elements to create something shiny and new.

Departing from the usual theme of street racing, Dominic (Vin Diesel) and Brian (Paul Walker), street racers and car thieves, decide to pull a heist of $100 million. It's supposed to be their "one

Fast Five

DIRECTED BY Justin Lin
WRITTEN BY Chris Morgan, Gary Scott Thompson (characters)
STARRING Vin Diesel, Paul Walker, Dwayne Johnson
RELEASED April 29, 2011
RATED PG-13

Showdown smackdown: When Federal agent Luke Hobbs (Dwayne "The Rock" Johnson) finally meets up with Dominic Toretto (Vin Diesel), it erupts in epic fisticuffs. Avco Embassy /Heritage Auctions

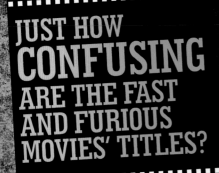

JUST HOW CONFUSING ARE THE FAST AND FURIOUS MOVIES' TITLES?

PART 1:
The Fast and the Furious

PART 2:
2 Fast 2 Furious

PART 3:
The Fast and the Furious: Tokyo Drift

PART 4:
Fast and Furious

PART 2:
Fast Five

POSSIBLE NAMES FOR PART 6:
Six Fast, Seven Furious, The F6st and the Furi6us, The Fasterest and the Furiousest.

last job" so they can retire and never have to steal anything again, which is generally movie code that one or more people will die on said heist. The quick and angry duo conjure up a plan to steal the money from a Rio crime lord, and to do so they gather a team of specialists comprised of their friends from the first four films and have a little fast and furious reunion.

Meanwhile, DSS agent Luke (Dwayne Johnson) searches for Dominic and Brian to arrest them for murders they've been framed for. The Rio crime lord isn't too keen on the duo either and sends his men to kill them seeing as how they've already stolen a very valuable car from him.

Fast Five is like *Ocean's Eleven's* street-racing, booty-shaking cousin, and I mean that in the most flattering way possible. This departure from the series typical race, rinse and repeat plotline breathes new life into it, and the return of fan favorite characters feels natural to the story, giving long-time fans a tasty reward for staying with the series for so long and making the movie itself feel like a street-racing equivalent of *The Avengers*.

Despite being a story with more maturity to it, *Fast Five* still retains some of those glorious, hormone-driven moments of adolescence that propelled the series in the first place. After all, it just wouldn't be a *Fast and Furious* film without gratuitous shots of scantily clad women lying all over cars, would it?

The action itself is frequent and varied. One minute there's a street race, the next a shootout (with rocket launchers), and the next is a hardcore one-on-one fight between Johnson and Diesel in what can only be described as "The Bald and the Built." The film's climax is nothing to sneeze at, either, as it's filled with classic heist movie misdirects and a chase scene involving a massive police vault being dragged through a city and being used as an automotive wrecking ball.

Fans will be happy to see the original main cast combine with people from all of the other films. Dwayne "The Rock" Johnson is a natural fit in the film and is no stranger to action. The writers really did a great job of bringing favorite elements from the previous films and creating them into a new, original film that still stays true to the *Fast and Furious* nature.

ELENA NEVES:
"Run, before it's too late. Leave Rio. You can be free."

DOMINIC TORETTO:
"Running ain't freedom. You should know that."

Michelle Rodriguez as daredevil Letty in *Fast and Furious.* Relativity Media/Universal/The Kobal Collection

MICHELLE RODRIGUEZ

Michelle Rodriguez has the acting chops to do whatever film she pleases, and it pleases me that she often chooses to play tough women in action roles. She's been on record stating how many times she's turned down typical roles such as "the girlfriend" or "the hostage" stating that, "I only wanna be someone I respect or someone that I consider interesting or fun. I'm here to entertain people and make a statement about female empowerment and strength …"

She certainly has done her part by always portraying strong women, often as characters tackling male-dominated professions. Case in point is her break-out role as the lead character in *Girlfight*, where she plays a troubled teen who takes up boxing. She then went on to kick ass in *Resident Evil, Avatar, S.W.A.T, Machete, Battle: Los Angeles,* and the fourth *Fast* movie: *Fast and Furious,* among several others. With her nuanced portrayal of such powerful women and her own personal resolve to choose roles because they're interesting, not just because they're available, Michelle Rodriguez helps prove that not all action stars are bad actors, and not all women are either a girlfriend or a hostage.

Resident Evil: Apocalypse

DIRECTED BY Alexander Witt
WRITTEN BY Paul W.S. Anderson
STARRING Milla Jovovich, Sienna Guillory, Eric Mabius
RELEASED September 10, 2004
RATED R

Nothing says good old-fashioned zombie action movie like having two women kick some zombie ass! *Resident Evil: Apocalypse* is the second of five films loosely based on the *Resident Evil* video games, emphasis on *loosely* seeing as how the main character of the films, Alice (Milla Jovovich), has nothing to do with the games. However, *Resident Evil: Apocalypse* does begin the series' trend of incorporating a few characters from the games per movie.

The first one establishes that Alice works for the Umbrella Corporation, the most powerful company in the world, as the head of security for an underground lab called The Hive. They were experimenting with viral weaponry when one of the viruses, the T-virus, gets out, killing everyone in The Hive. "Trouble was ... they didn't stay dead."

Beginning with the second film, the virus has made it above ground and is

ALICE:

"My name is Alice and I remember everything."

Davis Films/Impact Pictures

spreading all throughout Raccoon City, zombifying pretty much everyone. The officials close off the city to keep the virus from spreading and plan to nuke it the next morning after they grab a quick breakfast at Denny's. In doing so, they've also trapped many non-zombified people inside the city, including Alice. She joins forces with a few other survivors, one of whom is a character *actually* from the game, Jill Valentine (Sienna Guillory). They race against the clock to escape Raccoon City, all the while being attacked by zombies and other bizarre mutated creatures.

Resident Evil: Apocalypse isn't your typical zombie flick. In addition to the zombies, there are all kinds of mutants and undead critters running around tearing people to bits, like the Lickers, which use their oversized claws to climb walls and their massive, pointed tongues for stabbing their prey. There's also a pack of infected rottweilers ready to pounce on anything that looks like food. Possibly the scariest of them all, however, would be Nemesis, a gigantic, uber-powered undead monstrosity in a trenchcoat who occasionally favors having a rocket launcher, meaning that if he isn't crushing a person with his bare hands, he's blowing them into hell.

Resident Evil: Apocalypse entices audiences with zombie-fighting action, weird creatures, and two no-nonsense heroines who are just as good at gunning down zombies as they are in hand-to-hand combat, all of which make for 94 minutes of uncomplicated undead action.

Now that's how you make an entrance: Alice crashes through a stained-glass window of a church to save the people inside from Lickers. Davis Films/Impact Pictures/The Kobal Collection/Ralph Konow

The Bourne Series

DIRECTED BY Paul Greengrass, Doug Liman (The Bourne Identity)

WRITTEN BY Tony Gilroy (screenplay), W. Blake Herron (screenplay The Bourne Identity), Scott Z. Burns (screenplay, The Bourne Ultimatum), George Nolfi (screenplay, The Bourne Ultimatum) and Robert Ludlum (novels)

STARRING Matt Damon, Franka Potente, Chris Cooper, Joan Allen, Edgar Ramirez

RELEASED June 14, 2002 (The Bourne Identity)
July 23, 2004 (The Bourne Supremacy)
August 3, 2007 (The Bourne Ultimatum)

RATED R

In the *Bourne* film series, you've got assassins assassinating assassins all over the place, but one always triumphs over the others. His name is Bourne ... Jason Bourne (Matt Damon). They can shoot him, beat him, and run his car off a bridge into the river, but he'll still find a way to come back, exact his revenge, and make it to Grandma's house in time for dinner.

The first film in the series, *The Bourne Identity,* introduces poor little Bourne, who wakes up one day with not a clue as to who he is or how he got to be in the middle of the Mediterranean with two gun shot wounds to his back. For anyone else, retrograde amnesia wouldn't be life threatening; but for Bourne, not being able to remember that he's an assassin for the CIA who failed to complete his last mission can be lethal.

Hypnotic/Universal Pictures/Heritage Auctions

JASON BOURNE:

"I swear to God, if I even feel somebody behind me, there is no measure to how fast and how hard I will bring this fight to your doorstep. I'm on my own side now."

Scaling a building to escape is nothing compared to some of the other perils facing Jason Bourne on his quest to remember who he is. Hypnotic/Universal Pictures/Egon Endrenyi

The Bourne Supremacy continues Bourne's struggle to recover his memory and to live a normal life outside of the spy world, with *The Bourne Ultimatum* wrapping up his journey. Throughout the series, he fends off wave after wave of killers, all sent after him by the CIA in the hopes of covering up their dark secrets. Meanwhile, Bourne has been piecing together the truth about the now defunct

During an exciting high-speed chase in *The Bourne Supremacy*, Jason discovers Russian taxis are remarkably resilient. Universal/The Kobal Collection/Jay Maidment

Below, Jason discusses business with CIA internal investigator Pamela Landy (Joan Allen). Universal/Jasin Boland

CIA assassination program "Operation Treadstone," a program he was previously a member of, and all the while has to deal with the emergence of a new program, "Operation Blackbriar," sending agents to kill him.

The action in the *Bourne* series is much like a three-step program of ass-kicking increasing with each film, and by the time the viewer gets to the third film, the action has reached the apex of the pyramid. In fact, *The Bourne Ultimatum* wastes no time by beginning with the climactic action sequence from the end of the second film and from there the poop hits the fan and the splattered mess brings a film with

continuous pursuits on foot and in vehicles, and gritty close-contact fights.

The *Bourne* series is famous for its handheld style of camerawork and fast-paced action choreography, both of which often make for fights that are as confusing as real-life combat would be. And, yes, though the "shaki-cam" has been overdone recently, and does get tiresome during *Bourne*'s many conversations, it helps make for a unique style that's been often imitated in the years since.

PAMELA LANDY:

"Listen, people. Do you have any idea who you're dealing with? This is Jason Bourne. You are nine hours behind the toughest target you have ever tracked …"

THIS SUMMER JASON BOURNE COMES HOME

MATT DAMON

THE
BOURNE
ULTIMATUM

08·03·07

Conan the Barbarian

DIRECTED BY Marcus Nispel
WRITTEN BY Thomas Dean Donnelly
(story), Joshua Oppenheimer (story),
Sean Hood (story), Robert E. Howard
(character)
STARRING Jason Momoa, Ron Pearlman,
Rose McGowan
RELEASED August 19, 2011
RATED R

The making of the 2011 film *Conan the Barbarian* has caused some controversy because there are a lot of die-hard fans of the original *Conan the Barbarian* (1982) film. However, the 2011 film isn't a remake or a sequel; it's a new interpretation of the stories by Robert E. Howard. While many will always love the original film starring Arnold Schwarzenegger as Conan, the newest interpretation flies so much higher in terms of action and beats the hell out of a butt-ton more baddies!

Jason Momoa is Conan in the new *Conan the Barbarian*. This film is a true blue, split-you-down-the-middle-with-a-broadsword action movie. Conan is trained by his father (Ron Perlman) to be a fighter at a young age, and when Pop kicks the bucket at the hands of a group of warriors led by Khalar Zym (Stephen Lang) in front of kid Conan, he vows to get revenge. Years later, grown-up Conan goes on the hunt for Khalar Zym and leaves a trail of decapitated henchmen and beaten asses.

Conan the Barbarian's action grabs the audience by the loincloth and doesn't let go! The script probably has ten pages of dialogue to it; the rest is clashing swords and sand monsters. This formula describes it best: Fight, two minutes of talking, then a fight breaks out again, and then the cycle begins anew. Most of the combat is vicious, too, filled with the kind of dirty hand-to-hand brawls a person would only find in ancient times.

Because of the magnificent action, the plot and character growth do suffer somewhat … Okay, perhaps they're basically nonexistent. However, the film stays truer to the type of violence in Howard's books, as he is seen as the father of the

CONAN:
"I live, I love, I slay, and I am content."

Jason Momoa in the titular role of Conan slices and dices his way toward revenge.
Lionsgate/The Kobal Collection

"sword-and-sorcery" subgenre.

Here is what action movie freaks should expect from *Conan the Barbarian*: a hella fun time, lots of blood and gore, essentially non-stop action, and muscle-bound Jason Momoa with his shirt off the whole time! So give it a chance to stand on its own and don't let any comparisons to the original hold you back.

Lionsgate

Mission Impossible: Ghost Protocol

DIRECTED BY Brad Bird
WRITTEN BY Josh Appelbaum, André, Nemec, Bruce Geller (Mission: Impossible television series)
STARRING Tom Cruise, Jeremy Renner, Simon Pegg, Paula Patton
RELEASED December 23, 2011
RATED PG-13

ETHAN HUNT:
"Mission accomplished!"

Ethan Hunt (Tom Cruise) had better have good car insurance because he's going to need all the help he can get after *Mission Impossible: Ghost Protocol.* Every time he turns around, he's either wrecking a car himself, in a car that is crashing, or near some cars that are getting effed up. Maybe he's like kryptonite for cars, or maybe he's saved so much with Geico he just doesn't care. The world may never know.

Mission Impossible: Ghost Protocol is the fourth film of the *Mission: Impossible* series starring Tom Cruise as an I.M.F (Impossible Missions Force) agent. This time around, villain Cobalt (Michael Nyqvist), a Russian nuclear strategists (oooh, fancy!), decides that evolution isn't happening quickly enough and the world is being

Jeremy Renner hangs on tight to Tom Cruise during a precarious moment. Cruise performed all of his own stunts in the movie. Paramount Pictures/The Kobal Collection

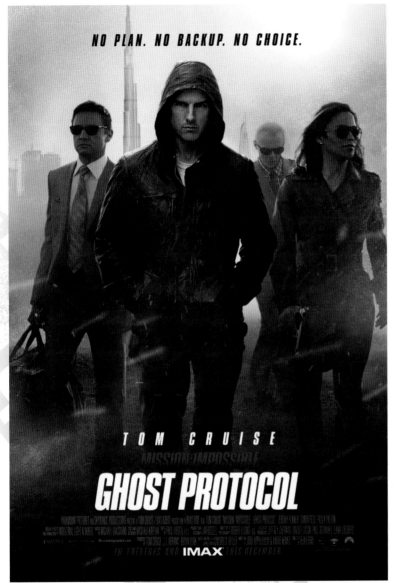

NO PLAN. NO BACKUP. NO CHOICE.

TOM CRUISE

MISSION IMPOSSIBLE

GHOST PROTOCOL

IMAX

Paramount Pictures

bogged down by weak humans. To help evolution move along a little faster, Cobalt decides to set off a nuclear bomb in the hopes that it will instigate a nuclear war between countries, with the logic that only the strong will survive such a war, and the rest of the weaklings will be scrubbed out of the gene pool.

Ethan Hunt and team are on to his plan like stink on poop. They've been framed by Cobalt for blowing up the Kremlin and are out to set the record straight and save humanity from nuclear war. Go team Hunt!

The fourth installment has all the roots of a great action film and even throws in a good story, something you'll be shocked to find out isn't always the most vital thing in action movies. More importantly, *Ghost Protocol* raises the bar on all the key qualities of an action film. There are authentic and creative action scenes in exquisite looking places. For example, instead of Hunt chasing the villain on a typical foot/car chase, they do it in a blinding sand storm, with Hunt having to constantly dodge cars and debris.

Bravo to Tom Cruise, Paula Patton, and Lea Seydoux, as they all decided to perform their own stunts in the most memorable scenes. Cruise scaled parts of the Burj Khalifa, the tallest building in the world, himself—no stunt doubles for him! And Patton and Seydoux participated in an all-out brawl against each other without using stunt doubles. The audience can really feel the waves of aggression emanating from them!

Ghost Protocol provides a fun stroll down action lane, surpassing the previous films in the series in every way.

Mad Max Beyond Thunderdome

DIRECTED BY George Miller, George Ogilvie
WRITTEN BY Terry Hayes, George Miller
STARRING Mel Gibson, Tina Turner, Bruce Spence
RELEASED July 10, 1985
RATED PG-13

Director George Miller handled the action scenes and stunts, while George Ogilvie directed the performances. Warner Bros./The Kobal Collection

Mad Max Beyond Thunderdome is the third film in the *Mad Max* series, a series set in a post-apocalyptic world where resources are scarce. After being robbed of everything he has to survive on, Mad Max (Mel Gibson) stumbles upon a town, Bartertown, with electricity and functioning technology made possible by an underground refinery that fuels everything with pig crap.

At this point, Mad Max has earned himself a reputation as an excellent fighter, so it's not long before the founder and head of the town, Aunty Entity (Tina Turner), seeks him out to strike a deal. She wants Max to challenge the head of the pig crap refinery's bodyguard, Blaster, to a duel. The head of the refinery, Master, has been using his position to challenge Aunty Entity's authority so she wants to take out his bodyguard, rendering Master unprotected and vulnerable. That's where the Thunderdome comes into play.

Two men enter, one man leaves! Anyone can challenge anyone to a fight in the Thunderdome without worrying about

Max strikes an alliance with Aunty Entity to help her get control of Bartertown. Warner Bros.

AUNTY ENTITY:

"Remember where you are. This is Thunderdome, and death is listening, and will take the first man that screams."

think he's there to save them and take them back to civilization … which he isn't since Bartertown is the only civilization nearby and it's no place for children. However, Max decides to help the children get their airplane ready to escape to somewhere better. Aunty, being simply the best, finds out and develops some escape plans of her own.

breaking any rules because … there are no rules! So Max agrees and challenges Blaster to a duel, and, like a good hero, he ultimately refuses to kill him, and Aunty throws Max out of the town and into the vast wasteland.

This is where the movie shifts a little bit and gets weird. Mad Max is saved by a group of children, reminiscent of the Lost Boys from *Peter Pan*, who

As far as the parts of good action movies go, one area that *Mad Max Beyond Thunderdome* scores big is the hero. Max is a guy with a hell of a rough past, as established by the first two movies, and with such a harsh world around him, it becomes all the more admirable that he continues to help others in need. Plus the man knows how to handle a weapon or two, and drives like a rabid dingo (but in a good way).

Mad Max Beyond Thunderdome also scores big in terms of quality action. The fight scene in the Thunderdome, an enclosed dome lined with jagged weapons like chainsaws and maces, is one of the most unique things about this installment in the *Mad Max* series, and it's put together in a way to really enhance the feeling of brutality.

The duel between Blaster (Paul Larsson) and Mad Max has some complex-looking choreography and makes fantastic use of the bungee cords each fighter has strapped to them, with both trying to use them to their advantage to fly around the arena and get the leg up on their opponent.

The whole series is also known for having excellent car chases, with each film ending with mass vehicle on vehicle combat, and this one is no different. A massive war between Aunty's people and Mad Max ignites, filled with crashes and explosions galore suitable for any action fan!

Aunty (Turner) and her band of merry rogues. Warner Bros.

Casino Royale

DIRECTED BY Martin Campbell
WRITTEN BY Neal Purvis (screenplay), Robert Wade (screenplay), Paul Haggis (screenplay), Sir Ian Fleming (novel)
STARRING Daniel Craig, Eva Green, Judi Dench
RELEASED November 17, 2006
RATED PG-13

Casino Royale, the 21st (!) film of the James Bond series, features the debut of Daniel Craig as the titular character. This was the start of a reboot for the franchise, with a new, fresh timeline starting at the beginning of Bond's career as a secret agent.

The first announcement of Craig being the new Bond caused a lot of controversy due to the contrast between his "look" and the look of previous Bonds. However, Craig changed critics' tune by magnificently portraying a darker, grittier Bond, one that's not the polite, well-rounded man brought forth by Pierce Brosnan and other previous actors. Craig's Bond is loose with his morality, bordering on sociopathic, and the fact that he's a member of MI6, a.k.a one of the good guys, seems almost incidental. But with a darker, grittier Bond comes a new type of action, with a greater emphasis on brutal, hand-to-hand combat and fast-paced gunplay.

Casino Royale opens with Bond earning his license to kill, becoming a full MI6 agent. Hungry for action, this newbie Bond starts investigating Le Chiffre (Mads Mikkelsen), who is suspected of financing terrorists. Hoping to bankrupt La Chiffre, Bond enters a high-stakes poker tournament being held by the villain, along the way meeting Vesper Lynd (Eva Green), a treasury employee sent to finance Bond's stake.

Action lovers will be blown away by the free-running sequence toward the beginning of the film, where Bond is chasing down a bomb maker portrayed by Sebastien Foucan, and the two hoof it on a Parkour-style footrace across a construction site. The scene was inspired by one deleted from an earlier Bond movie, *On Her Majesty's Secret Service,* and it's a fantastic display of finesse versus brawn. The bomb maker moves with almost inhuman agility, something that Bond simply cannot match, so instead he uses his brawn to power through obstacles rather than over them. Case in point, when the bomb maker leaps through a tiny gap above a section of drywall, Bond plows through it like a bear looking for honey. This scene does a marvelous job getting the audience accustomed to this new Bond's personality, showcasing his propensity for powerhouse brutality over the sleek manners of the Bonds of old.

Daniel Craig gave a shot of adrenaline to the *Bond* franchise with his portrayal of the spy. Eon/Danjaq/Sony/Heritage Auctions

VESPER LYND:

"It doesn't bother you? Killing all those people?"

JAMES BOND:

"Well, I wouldn't be very good at my job if it did."

"Well, I understand Double-O's have a very short life expectancy...."

—JAMES BOND

Transporter 2

DIRECTED BY Louis Leterrier
WRITTEN BY Luc Besson, Robert Mark Kamen
STARRING Jason Statham, Amber Valetta, Kate Nauta
RELEASED September 2, 2005
RATED PG-13

Need something delivered? Frank Martin is the guy to call. For those "I'm sorry" flowers that need to reach a special someone within the hour or they'll be on a plane to Paris, Frank's the guy. For all of the dirty magazines, toys, and tapes that need to go bye bye before the parents come for an extended stay, call Frank. For the post bank heist getaway driver, Frank Martin will be there, no names, no details, no questions asked!

Transporter 2 is more of the exact same stuff as the first one, only ramped up a 100 times. Frank Martin (Jason Statham) tries to get away from transporting illegal items by becoming a chauffeur for a rich family, and in doing so, bonds with both the son and the husband's ignored, hot wife. Chauffeuring doesn't prove to be any safer of a job, however, because a posse of bad guys kidnap the little boy and inject him with a deadly virus that spreads to

Lola (Nauta) and Frank (Statham) in one of their face offs, the result of which doesn't turn out as pretty as she is.
Europacorp/TF1 Corp/The Kobal Collection

Euroupacorp/TFI Corp

FRANK MARTIN:

"I'm afraid that your flight's been canceled."

GIANNI:

"I'm afraid that YOU have been canceled!"

realm of realism, *Transporter 2* says, "To hell with that" and kicks things up a notch, giving us things like Frank ramping his car off of something, spiraling it through the air just right to scrape a bomb off of the bottom using a hook and crane. All this happens just in time for the bomb to blow up, with him a safe distance away.

Another point that amps up *Transporter 2* is the eye candy for everyone! If you like men, Jason Statham is ripped and constantly taking his shirt off. If you like women, Kate Nauta plays a psychotic villain who is constantly running around in lingerie. She and Statham can have a battle of the abs because they are both cut like a freakin' Ginsu knife.

For a crazy fun action-filled time, action movie freaks should watch *Transporter 2*. Actually, the first one is worth watching as well, even though it doesn't have the same level of crazy "that could never happen" action. It's still chock full of greatness, but the second one takes it a step further and explodes a lot harder. (Some feel that the third one is kind of a letdown, though, so it may be best to leave *The Transporter* as a duology instead of a trilogy).

everyone he breathes on. That posse kidnapped the wrong kid. Now, Frank must save the kid and find the antidote for the virus before it becomes an epidemic.

Although *The Transporter* (2002) is an incredible film filled with a lot of action, *Transporter 2* takes some of those same elements, kicks subtlety to the curb, and instead fills its running time with an over-the-top frenzy of action. Between action sequences, there's literally a four-minute breather before something else pulse-pounding gets started, just enough time for Frank to change locales (and maybe clothes) before he starts stomping some asses again.

Where *The Transporter* tries to keep things somewhat within the

Terminator 2: Judgment Day

DIRECTED BY James Cameron
WRITTEN BY James Cameron, William Wisher
STARRING Arnold Schwarzenegger, Linda Hamilton, Edward Furlong, Robert Patrick
RELEASED July 3, 1991
RATED R

The Terminator protects his young charge, John, who is the hope for humanity.
Carolco/Heritage Auctions

The Terminator (Arnold Schwarzenegger) said he'd be back and boy was he right. *Terminator 2: Judgment Day (T2)* features twice as many terminators as the first one, a.k.a. two, causing the creativity of the action to go sky high as the chance of survival plummets for everyone.

In *The Terminator*, viewers learn that Sarah Connor (Linda Hamilton) will eventually give birth to John Connor, the boy who will grow up to be the leader of the human Resistance against Skynet, an artificial intelligence system that will become self-aware and try to wipe out the human race.

T2 begins with a ten-year-old John Connor, whose mother has been preparing him since birth for the war against Skynet. Forget baseball cards or video games, this kid is getting hand grenades and M16s for his birthday. Even with all of his preparation, however, John isn't quite ready when a T-1000 (Robert

Beneath the Terminator's human-like exterior lies a powerful metal endoskeleton.
Carolco/Heritage Auctions

Patrick) terminator shows up from the future to try to kill him. Terminators–always ruining everything.

Future John knows he won't be ready, so he sends the Terminator (Arnold Schwarzenegger), a T-800 model, back in time to protect young John. Geez, couldn't he have spent a few extra Future Bucks on a newer model? It's just his future existence and the fate of humanity depending on it, but whatever. So the Terminator sets out to protect John and Sarah from the T-1000, all to ensure what little

IT'S NOTHING PERSONAL.

TERMINATOR 2
JUDGMENT DAY

ASSAR Presents A PACIFIC WESTERN Production In Association With LIGHTSTORM ENTERTAINMENT A JAMES CAMERON Film ARNOLD SCHWARZENEGGER
ATOR 2: JUDGMENT DAY" LINDA HAMILTON ROBERT PATRICK
D BUFF MARK GOLDBLATT, A.C.E. RICHARD A. HARRIS Music Brad Fiedel
Executive GALE ANNE HURD and MARIO KASSAR Production JOSEPH NEMEC, III Makeup and STAN WINSTON Computer Graphics by INDUSTRIAL LIGHT & MAGIC
Producers Director of ADAM GREENBERG, A.S.C. Co-Producers B.J. RACK and STEP
Written by JAMES CAMERON & WILLIAM WISHER Produced and Directed by JAMES CAM

COMING THIS

hope humanity has against Skynet.

Terminator 2 may be one of the most well known and critically acclaimed action movies in the world. And why wouldn't it be? It has Arnold in top form, playing a machine gradually learning what it is to be human. Against him there's Robert Patrick as T-1000, one of the most feared and powerful villains ever to grace the silver screen, and Patrick gives an intimidating performance as this nigh-unkillable monstrosity. Caught between them is Linda Hamilton as Sarah Connor, a woman hardened by war and struggling to maintain some sense of her own humanity.

If there's two things terminators are known for, it's never stopping, and never showing mercy, something that *Terminator 2* takes to heart in its action scenes. This movie shows no mercy in generating a beautiful action extravaganza, with the T-1000 destroying anything in its path. If a person doesn't have the last name of Connor, they're pretty much screwed. And since the Connors always have terminators after them, they're pretty much screwed, too. So, really, if there's ever a terminator present, RUN, BITCH, RUN!

T2 is easily the best film out of the Terminator series. It has amazing action sequences, special effects that were mind-blowing at the time and still hold up to this day, and top-notch character development. While the first film is definitely worth a watch, and *Terminator 3* and *4* (*Terminator: Salvation*) each have their selling points, *T2* is the embodiment of the perfect terminator film. You cannot be called an action movie freak without having this one under your belt, so watch this movie if you want to live.

In the future, the machines rise up. Carolco/Heritage Auctions

Mano a metal: The T-800 (Schwarzenegger) confronts the T-1000 (Patrick). Carolco/Heritage Auctions

Sarah Connor transforms from timid victim in the first movie to full-out warrior in *T2*. Carolco/Heritage Auctions

Sarah Connor's reputation as an infamous badass started with Linda Hamilton (and writers James Cameron and William Wisher, Jr., of course). She's a fighter, through and through, having spent much of her life protecting and nurturing her pup of a son so that one day he can hopefully grow into the future savior of mankind, all while occasionally battling off metal-hearted machines. That woman deserves a medal … and a vacation.

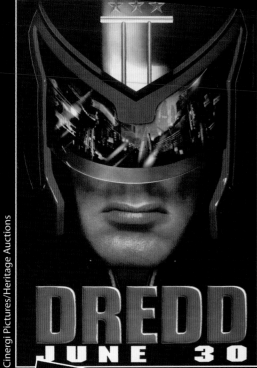

DREDD

JUNE 30

IT'S TIME FOR "ACTION"

NAME: Jericho Jackson.
NICKNAME: "Action".
HOME: Detroit.
PROFESSION: Cop.
EDUCATION: Harvard Law.
HOBBY: Fighting Crime.

WEAPON: You're looking at 'em.

CARL WEATHERS
is
ACTION JACKSON

LORIMAR FILM ENTERTAINMENT PRESENTS
A SILVER PICTURES PRODUCTION
CARL WEATHERS "ACTION JACKSON" CRAIG T. NELSON
VANITY · SHARON STONE · THOMAS F. WILSON
MUSIC HERBIE HANCOCK WITH MICHAEL KAMEN
PHOTOGRAPHY MATTHEW F. LEONETTI A.S.C.
DIRECTED BY ROBERT RENEAU PRODUCED BY JOEL SILVER
WRITTEN BY CRAIG R. BAXLEY

WILL SMITH   KEVIN KLINE

WILD WILD WEST

IT'S A WHOLE NEW WEST.

BRUCE WILLIS

HUDSON HAWK

Danger is his middle name.

IN BRIGHTEST DAY.
IN BLACKEST NIGHT.

GREEN LANTERN

COMING SOON
IN 3D

NICOLAS CAGE

GHOST RIDER
SPIRIT OF VENGEANCE

THE GRISTLE

Action Movies That Weren't As Good As They Should Have Been

How's the burger meal so far? Pretty tasty, right? All of the ingredients have combined together to make something oh-so very delicious? Good. Sometimes it doesn't work out, though. Sometimes things come out yucky even when you were expecting something good. That's when you know you're not biting into a delicious burger ... but a huge chunk of gristle. Here are some films that were expected to be great, but ended up being big fat chunks of gristle instead.

- Wild Wild West
- Action Jackson
- Judge Dredd
- Ghost Rider: Spirit of Vengeance
- Hudson Hawk
- Green Lantern
- Ecks Vs. Sever
- Ultraviolet
- Elektra
- Batman & Robin
- Speed 2

- Punisher: War Zone
- Last Action Hero
- Hunt to Kill
- Starship Troopers 2: Hero of the Federation
- Max Payne
- The Matrix: Reloaded
- The Matrix: Revolutions
- Jonah Hex
- Battlefield Earth
- Sucker Punch

MARK WAHLBERG
MAX PAYNE

20th Century Fox

113

Columbia Pictures/Heritage Auctions

20th Century Fox/Marvel/Heritage Auctions

Lionsgate/Marvel Knights

Screen Gems/Heritage Auctions

Warner Bros./Heritage Auctions

20th Century Fox/Heritage Auctions

114

MATRIX
RELOADED
MAY 15 2003

MATRIX
REVOLUTIONS
NOVEMBER 5

Village Roadshow Pictures/Warner Bros./
Heritage Auctions

Village Roadshow Pictures/
Warner Bros./Heritage
Auctions

TriStar Pictures

STARSHIP
TROOPERS 2
Hero Of The Federation

They're coming back to wipe us out!

Legendary Pictures/DC Comics

JOSH BROLIN   MEGAN FOX
JONAH HEX
2010

A MIND-BENDING VISION OF REALITY FROM THE DIRECTOR OF 'WATCHMEN' & '300'
YOU WILL BE UNPREPARED

SUCKER PUNCH

Warner Bros.

MARCH 25
EXPERIENCE IT IN IMAX

STEVE AUSTIN
HUNT TO KILL

SURVIVAL OF THE BADDEST

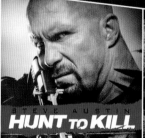

Nasser Group

115

Taking inspiration from more than 100 other action movies, *Hot Fuzz* follows two police officers trying to solve mysterious deaths in a small English village.
Focus Features/Heritage Auctions

THE CHEESE
Parodies

It's time to add some cheese to this action burger! Every genre has them, everybody loves them … it's the parodies! Parodies bring attention to the most common themes of a genre by exploiting them, and in the process remind us why we love the genre so much in the first place. Nothing is safe; even the most serious, heartbreaking moments can be spun on their heads and transformed into a comedy gold mine if done correctly (although when done incorrectly, the entire thing becomes ridiculously painful, like getting a root canal while watching a tape of your elderly grandparents getting it on).

Parody films are common to each genre, which begs the question: what makes one parody rise above the rest? A good starting point is to know the exact film elements to parody. For instance, the action hero having magic guns with infinite bullets, or leaping down ten stories and being okay because they rolled at the end of the fall, or getting shot in the arm several times but still being able to use it like nothing happened are all things that run rampant in action films. And, generally, the audience accepts these things. After all, this is an *action* hero we're talking about, these guys (and gals) are freakin' tough.

Parodies, however, take those things and exaggerate them a 100 times. Rambo shoots fifty shots without reloading? The Rambo parody has to shoot five thousand. Jason Statham just jumped out of a helicopter and lived? The Statham parody can jump from a space shuttle and survive re-entering the Earth's atmosphere.

Parodies make up the cheese on the burger because they're close

to the meat of what makes an action film, but executed differently. And you know what? Cheese isn't for everyone. Some are lactose intolerant, or some think parody movies are simply ridiculous, but parodies add some levity to the seriousness of their chosen genre. Action movie parodies have been making people laugh with scenes of chickens fired from bows, people surviving grenades to the face, and meta jokes about action movie tropes for many, many years.

One of the villains The Chosen One (Steve Oedekerk) encounters on his quest in *Kung Pow! Enter the Fist*, is Moo Nieu, a cow gifted at karate and who squirts her milk as a weapon. Fox Animation/ Peter Lovino

Black Dynamite

DIRECTED BY Scott Sanders
WRITTEN BY Scott Sanders (screenplay), Michael Jai White (screenplay/story), Byron Minns (screenplay/story)
STARRING Michael Jai White, Salli Richardson, Arsenio Hall, Kevin Chapman, Tommy Davidson
RELEASED Oct. 16, 2009
RATED R

Dyno-mite! Dyno-mite! Tired of feelin' like a jive-ass turkey all the time? Well, step up your game by watching *Black Dynamite.* This film'll teach you how to talk the talk, but you gotta walk the walk on your own, baby.

A man with a powder-blue suit, super 'fro, and his own badass theme song, Black Dynamite (Michael Jai White) is a Kung fu master who don't take no shit from no-one! When he learns that his brother was murdered, and that his streets are being flooded with a drug that's putting kids in the hospital, he goes on a warpath of vengeance the likes of which this world has never seen! During his investigations, Black Dynamite unfolds a massive web of deceit that goes all the way to the top! He finds that the drug dealers responsible for his brother's death are selling a malt liquor that will literally emasculate a man by shrinking his, uh, manhood. Unable to fight the battle against small penises alone, he enlists the help of some of his brothas from otha mothas.

Black Dynamite is a parody of the 1970s blaxploitation films, and it's an absolute masterpiece. All the elements of a blaxploitation film are brought to life, from pimps and hos to the negative portrayal of white people and the studly and smooth, ultra Kung fu master, eponymous hero himself, Black Dynamite. This film is just bursting with little detailed bits of tongue-in-cheek goodness, like the boom microphone occasionally dropping down into the shot

BLACK DYNAMITE:

"Innocents to be defended, Black Dynamite will be there, delivering ass-whuppings. And I will not hesitate to lay the hammer down on any clown that comes around."

(complete with the actors trying not to notice it), and actors saying part of the stage directions as if it was dialogue, all of which really add to the blaxploitation feeling. The filmmakers were so thorough in their parody that they even filmed the movie using Super 16 cameras, giving it that authentic high-contrasted, over-saturated coloration that was common to '70s films.

This film is one that needs to be watch repeatedly, because audiences will be laughing so hard over the first joke that the next three will get missed. Not content to be simply a comedy, though, *Black Dynamite* sprinkles some great action sequences in the mix, thanks in no small part to the martial arts prowess of star Michael Jai White. So, in the words of Black Dynamite's hombre, Bullhorn, gather 'round, you suckas, and check the smoothest baddest motha to EVER hit the big screen, Black Dynamite! *Dyno-mite! Dyno-mite!*

Black Dynamite (Michael Jai White) has women literally falling at his feet. Ars Nova/The Kobal Collection

Kung Pow! Enter the Fist

DIRECTED/WRITTEN BY Steve Oedekerk
STARRING Steve Oedekerk, Fei Lung, Leo Lee
RELEASED January 25, 2002
RATED PG-13

Action movie freaks with a love of Hong Kong martial arts films will get a kick out of *Kung Pow! Enter the Fist,* a parody of a genre full of action ... goofy, often bizarre action, but action nonetheless.

Kung Pow! Enter the Fist uses footage from Hong Kong film *Tiger and Crane Fist* and mixes it with original footage to form a bizarre hybrid of old and new. *Kung Pow's* story centers around The Chosen One (Steve Oedekerk), a man who wanders around from town to town in search of Master Pain, a.k.a Betty, the squawky-voiced psychopath who murdered his parents and *tried* to kill him the night he was born. The Chosen One stops for a bit at Master Tang's dojo to sharpen his fighting skills when Master Pain arrives at the exact same town, and the two end up on a collision course.

Kung Pow is a parody on multiple levels; fans of martial arts films

The Chosen One (Oedekerk) comes away with a little more than victory after an encounter with some bad guys. Fox Animation/The Kobal Collection/Peter Lovino

Fox Animation

MASTER BETTY:

"Well, I thought you looked familiar. Sorry, I didn't recognize you without crap in your pants!"

will appreciate the tongue-in-cheek use in the kinds of close-ups and camera tricks typical of the genre, or the deliberately poor syncing of dialogue with mouth movements, or even some of the strange mannerisms and motions of the actors in some of these old martial arts movies. At one point, an old man is in bed, apparently dying, while another old man vigorously rubs his chest and talks to him. *Kung Pow!* uses the footage for laughs, but you can't help but wonder what the hell was supposed to be happening in *Tiger and Crane Fist.*

On the flip side, anyone without a background in martial arts movies can enjoy the utter weirdness of the rest of the film. It has Kung fu cows, thugs getting holes punched in their chests, and talking tongues. And that's just the tip of the iceberg.

Kung Pow! Enter the Fist is Steven Oedekerk's one-man movie. In addition to his role as director, producer, writer, and star, he also provided the voices for nearly every character, from the obnoxious Wimp-Lo to the Miss Piggy-esque Ling.

Loaded Weapon 1

DIRECTED BY Gene Quintano
WRITTEN BY Don Holley (story/screenplay), Tori Tellem (story), Gene Quintano (screenplay)
STARRING Emilio Estevez, Samuel L. Jackson, Jon Lovitz
RELEASED February 5, 1993
RATED PG-13

If you think *Loaded Weapon 1* is an action film about buddy cops starring a loose cannon played by Mel Gibson and a straight-laced cop played by Danny Glover, well, you're kind of right. It's a parody of one of the most well-known buddy cop films, *Lethal Weapon,* and stars Samuel L. Jackson and Emilio Estevez spoofing characters Roger Murtaugh and Martin Riggs, respectively.

Fans of the *Lethal Weapon* series can enjoy this satire that is overflowing with references big and small to their favorite action films. *Loaded Weapon* isn't just a straight play by play of *Lethal Weapon,* though, throwing in spoofs of *Basic Instinct, Silence of the Lambs, Rambo, Die Hard,* and of course, *Dirty Harry,* much like the modern "comedy" films like *Epic Movie,* only *Loaded Weapon 1* is actually, you know, *funny*, and has actual jokes written in rather than being content to coast by spoofing movie scene after movie scene.

In *Loaded Weapon 1,* Wes Luger (Jackson) is looking to avenge his former partner's murder and is paired up with unpredictable Jack Colt (Estevez) in order to do so. Colt just lost a partner himself (a canine partner) driving him to the brink of insanity so the two must learn to trust each other and work together to solve Luger's former partner's death. Along the way, the duo faces off against drug dealers, criminal masterminds, and ... *William Shatner.*

This parody is lighter on the action than most of the others, but what it lacks in action it makes up for with famous cameos. It also does a great job of blending in the more obscure jokes with the obvious ones, giving true action movie freaks a little something extra to giggle about.

(Oh, and in case you're wondering, there is no *Loaded Weapon 2.*)

Sgt. Billie York (Whoopie Goldberg) at the mercy of a mime with a finger gun. New Line/The Kobal Collection

WES LUGER:
"We're investigating a felony, Miss Demeanor."

Hot Shots! Part Deux

DIRECTED BY Jim Abrahams
WRITTEN BY Jim Abrahams, Pat Proft
STARRING Charlie Sheen, Lloyd Bridges, Valeria Golino
RELEASED May 31, 1993
RATED PG-13

In *Hot Shots! Part Deux,* a parody of *Rambo,* Charlie Sheen reprises his role as Topper Harley, former jet pilot turned monk/bareknuckle brawler. Sheen reportedly worked out eight hours a day in order to pull off a convincing Rambo-esque hero, and his efforts definitely pay off. So what does every action hero need? A hype man! Rambo has his former commander Colonel Trautman portrayed by Richard Crenna, and Topper has Colonel Walters, portrayed by Richard Crenna. That's right, Crenna is playing a parody of his own character. Gotta respect a man for being able to have fun with himself. Wait, that didn't sound right …

In the film, Saddam Hussein (Jerry Haleva) has captured American soldiers, so a rescue team is called on to invade Hussein's residence and set the prisoners free. When those guys are captured, another rescue squad is called in to rescue everyone, this time led by Colonel Walters. When *those* guys get captured, Topper has no choice but to wade back into battle and rescue his comrades.

When it comes to improvising in the middle of a fight, Topper is a true pro. When he runs out of ammo, he kills his

Topper buries himself in a limitless supply of bullets. 20th Century Fox/The Kobal Collection

enemies by throwing bullet casings at them. And when there's no more ammo to throw, he uses a bow and arrow. And when he runs out of arrows, he uses a chicken. And when there are no more chickens to walk the earth, he kills the baddies by tightening their ties around their necks!

Hot Shots! Part Deux is a parody in the vein of *Airplane!* and the *Naked Gun* films, meaning the audience can expect Looney Toons-style physical comedy, puns so numerous you'll go cross-eyed, and the occasional fourth-wall breaking cameo, including one from another actor known for playing a military hero.

20th Century Fox

THE BODY COUNT COUNTDOWN!

A film can't be a proper spoof of the *Rambo* series unless it can dish out an absurdly high body count, and *Hot Shots! Part Deux* delivers with a total of 114. But how do some of your other favorite action movies stack up?

1.	First Blood	**1**
2.	Die Hard	**20**
3.	Lethal Weapon	**26**
4.	Mad Max 2: Road Warrior	**44**
5.	Rambo: First Blood Part II	**67**
6.	The Long Kiss Goodnight	**68**
7.	Total Recall	**77**
8.	Kill Bill Vol 1	**95**
9.	Missing in Action	**100**
10.	Resident Evil: Apocalypse	**123**
11.	Dawn of the Dead (2004)	**131**
12.	The Wild Bunch	**145**
13.	The Chronicles of Riddick	**187**
14.	Bullet in the Head	**214**
15.	Rambo	**247**
16.	Starship Troopers	**256**
17.	Hard Boiled	**307**
18.	Troy	**572**
19.	300	**600**
20.	Lord of the Rings: Return of the King	**836**

Hot Fuzz

DIRECTED BY Edgar Wright
WRITTEN BY Edgar Wright, Simon Pegg
STARRING Simon Pegg, Nick Frost
RELEASED February 14, 2007 (Ireland)
RATED R

Over a hundred action films were used as inspiration when Edgar Wright and Simon Pegg wrote the script for *Hot Fuzz*. While it may not technically be classified as a parody, it absolutely takes cues from other action films and acts as a deconstruction of the genre by breaking down and drawing attention to themes common to action movies. For example, naïve, inexperienced cop Danny Butterman (Nick Frost) asks these questions of experienced officer Nicholas Angel (Simon Pegg): "Have you ever fired two guns whilst leaping backwards through the air? Have you ever fired a gun whilst on a high speed pursuit? Is it true that there's a spot in a man's head that if you shoot it, it will explode?"

Even though *Hot Fuzz* brings attention to these action clichés, by the end of the film the two officers have done almost all of them. However, rather than doing everything as a mockery of the clichés, it is instead done as more of a respectful, tongue-in-cheek tribute to everything from *Point Break* to *Bad Boys II*.

Officer Nicholas Angel is a good cop, perhaps the best. He's so good, in fact, that it makes his commanding officers look like lazy pieces of crap, and so they transfer him to a slower paced, "crime free" village where he finds himself partnered up with action movie aficionado Danny Butterman. The lack of concern his new police department exhibits toward petty crimes is annoying to Nicholas, who has spent his life doing everything exactly by the books.

On the edge of dying from boredom thanks to the lack of real crime in the village, things start to look up for Nicholas as mysterious murders start happening, giving the expert cop something to use his talents on and his newbie partner a chance to live out the action movies he loves so dearly.

The team of Wright, Pegg, and Frost are a three-headed juggernaut of comedy and storytelling. Like the team's previous film, *Shaun of the Dead, Hot Fuzz* is a movie written with a sharp awareness of the genre's tropes, and they're employed or averted with great effect.

One of the more unique strengths of the film is that they didn't pigeonhole a female love interest into it. Nicholas did have one in the first draft of the script but she was cut, and most of her dialogue was given to Danny completely unchanged.

The last 45 minutes or so of this film is continuous excitement between the murders, chases, and fights. While the first half is a bit on the slow side, mostly focusing on comedy rather than action, the fish and chips hit the wall for the third act with a series of shootouts and chase scenes that would make John Woo blush.

Angel and Butterman do the ol' backward leap-and-fire maneuver. Focus Features/The Kobal Collection

NICHOLAS ANGEL:
"I don't remember a time when I didn't want to be a police officer ... apart from the summer of 1979 when I wanted to be Kermit the Frog."

BEST
SELF-INFLICTED INCAPACITATION!

Nicholas is squaring off against Simon Skinner (Timothy Dalton) in a miniature replica of the town. After Nicholas thinks he's won the fight, he begins to walk away, but as soon as he does, Skinner leaps out with a box cutter in his hand and a blood-curdling scream in his throat. He charges toward Nicholas but ends up tripping over a miniature truck, stumbling, and falling onto the mini-church's spiked steeple, impaling himself under the chin and out of his mouth.

The legendary Bruce Lee in a scene from *Enter the Dragon*. Concord/Warner Bros./Heritage Auctions

THE LETTUCE
Martial Arts

Sometimes using a gun is just too easy. Sometimes you just want to get in there and do some damage, man to man (or woman to man), fist-to-face style. That's where martial arts films come in. Martial artists don't need to carry a weapon because they are the weapon!

Martial arts movies are to the action genre what lettuce is to the hamburger: they're a crisp, clean addition to something tasty, and they're good for you. Martial artists display amazing control over their movements, and with a wide range of fighting styles at their disposal, you'll see everything from the veering, lurching style of drunken boxing to the brutality of Muay Thai fighters decimating their foes with a single deadly elbow to the face.

Martial arts movies are extra impressive because they generally have real people executing real moves with their bodies, moves that, if you practice long and hard enough, you might be able to do, too. That may be one of the martial arts genre's biggest drawing factors—the fact that the only thing separating you from the badass onscreen is years of practice. In this way, martial arts are self-sustaining; kids watch movies of martial artists kicking ass and grow up to become martial arts masters themselves. Just ask any martial artist over the age of thirty why they studied martial arts and their answers will probably all be the same: "I saw Bruce Lee do it, and I wanted to do it, too."

Guys like Bruce Lee, Jackie Chan, and Chuck Norris are some of history's most enduring martial arts performers, thanks to their abilities to act decently enough and throw a roundhouse kick to the face of anyone who crosses them. After all, doesn't everyone get a warm and fuzzy feeling after seeing Chuck Norris masterfully annihilate the opponent with a round house kick to the face? "You have the right (kick) to remain silent!"

So if you're looking for some lettuce to top off your action hamburger, then look no further than the following films, which are some of the most stupendous, face-rocking martial arts flicks action freaks will ever find.

A disillusioned assassin (Rain) looks for retribution against his former mentor in *Ninja Assassin*.
Warner Bros. Pictures

129

Enter the Dragon

DIRECTED BY Robert Clouse
WRITTEN BY Michael Allin
STARRING Bruce Lee, John Saxon, Jim Kelly
RELEASED August 19, 1973
RATED R

You don't need a weapon when your fists are the weapon. Concord/Warner Bros./Heritage Auctions

LEE:
"Why doesn't somebody pull out a .45 and, bang, settle it?"

Not even a Wolverine-like paw can stop Lee from taking down the bad guy. Concord/Warner Bros./Heritage Auctions

One of the competitors tries to make an opponent say "Uncle." Concord/Warner Bros./Heritage Auctions

If, for some crazy reason, you don't know who Bruce Lee is, allow me to present you with a simple rule to follow when watching this movie: whenever you see a rock-hard wall of abs and biceps so defined they'll cut you like a Jedi Knight's light saber, that's Bruce Lee!

In *Enter the Dragon*, Bruce Lee plays Lee, a creatively named master of Shaolin martial arts. Once the police learn of a martial arts tournament being held on a secluded island owned by Han (Shih Kien), a former Shaolin student, they ask Lee to go undercover for them as they suspect Han is involved with prostitution and drug dealing but can't perform any investigations on the island because it's out of their jurisdiction.

But kicking ass in an island martial arts tournament? That's right smack dab in the middle of Bruce's jurisdiction.

Bruce Lee starts the film showing off his supreme martial arts skills, and follows up by espousing a few of his fighting philosophies. The guy's got enough brains, skills, and swagger all mixed

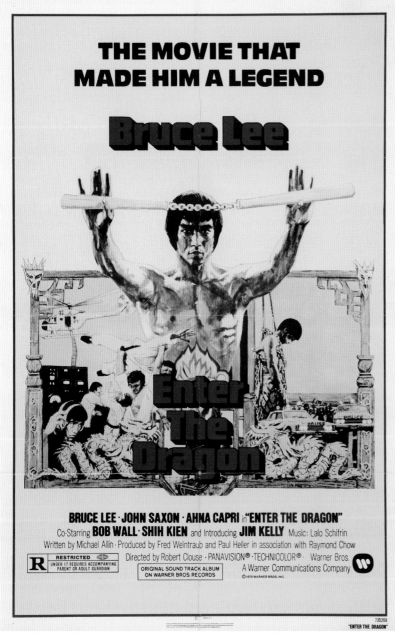

Concord/Warner Bros./Heritage Auctions

together to give him an air of ultimate badassery. He's even a bit of a teacher, too, educating his students on things like "Never take your eye off your enemy even when bowing," and "Feel, don't think." He outsmarts his opponents with his martial arts style of "fighting without fighting." Excuse me! Let me correct myself: He outsmarts people trying to fight him. "There is no opponent, because the word 'I' does not exist."

Everything Lee does is badass in *Enter the Dragon*, but I especially love the part where he shows up for a fighting event wearing his own clothing instead of the required uniform. One guy asks him why he isn't in uniform, and Lee doesn't even answer; he just gives him a look that says, "I will kill you if you question me again," and the guy scampers off. Do not question the Lee!

Enter the Dragon has been incredibly influential in the United States, inspiring others to learn martial arts as well as make martial arts movies. And for good reason, too, as it was a groundbreaking display of martial arts choreography. There are plenty of amazing fight scenes, one of which features a young extra named Jackie Chan, but the finale is what really breaks into crazy awesome territory – an all-out brawl between, literally, four hundred billion martial artists.

While *Enter the Dragon* is a classic, it's also one of the first, and most well-known, martial arts movies in the Western world. It was the first Chinese martial arts film to be produced by a major Hollywood studio and was selected for preservation in the National Film Registry. It's also the last film Lee was in before his death, and a fantastic note to go out on.

BRUCE LEE

What can be said about Bruce Lee that hasn't already been said? The man's a legend and an inspiration to just about every other martial artist in the world who followed in his footsteps. Lee may have only been alive for 32 years, but he left a long-lasting legacy that changed the world of martial arts and cinema forever. It's because of his incredible expertise that America became aware of the power and possibilities of martial arts. In fact, it's been argued that if it weren't for Lee, the Western world may have never been as influenced and saturated with martial arts as it is today.

After getting beat up by a gang, a young Lee decided to learn martial arts to protect himself. He studied Wing Chun Kung fu for five years under Sifu Yip Man, then went on to create his own school of martial arts/philosophy, Jeet Kune Do a.k.a "the art of fighting without fighting," and opened many training schools in California. The man has a lifetime of acting experiences under his belt, having been in films since he was a baby, but his most notable roles came as an adult. He landed the role of Kato, Green Hornet's sidekick, in the television series *The Green Hornet*. His prowess and undeniable swagger impressed all the right people and soon he was

Iconic legend Bruce Lee shows off his brilliant martial arts prowess in still shots from *Enter the Dragon*. Concord/Warner Bros./The Kobal Collection

swaggering onto the big screen, beating up bad guys and dishing out life lessons, all the while looking like a total badass. Though he only made a few films in his short adult life, the physical feats he displayed were so amazing that they've left a powerful legacy.

Lee personally gave lessons to Steve McQueen and James Coburn, two U.S. actors famous for their action films. Chuck Norris also studied Jeet Kune Do and all three men were some of the pallbearers at Lee's funeral. Many modern athletes, martial artists, and actors have cited Bruce Lee as their inspiration to get into martial arts. If this is the kind of legacy Lee left behind after just a few years in the film industry, imagine what would have happened had he lived. However, as it is, he left the world when he was in peak physical condition, never having to suffer the ravages that time would have taken on his body, or negative reviews of any of his movies, or the paparazzi going through his trashcans to see what he ate the night before.

Opening the eyes of the Western world to martial arts encouraged numerous people to study the sport and become talented martial artists themselves, many of whom went on to create some of history's greatest action movies, and all because a boy named Bruce didn't want to get beaten up anymore. Thanks, Bruce, for changing lives and the world of entertainment.

Ip Man

DIRECTED BY Wilson Yip
WRITTEN BY Edmond Wong (screenplay)
STARRING Donnie Yen, Simon Yam, Siu-Wong Fan
RELEASED December 12, 2008
RATED R

Ip Man is loosely based on the life of a real Chinese martial artist, a man who taught many renowned martial artists including the legendary Bruce Lee himself. The film is a fantastic display of what these men are capable of, with fights breaking out all throughout the film and the combatants using different martial arts styles.

Usually in an action movie, the hero gets ground down and has to rise up to overcome an opponent greater than he is, and along the way he has to struggle to do what needs to be done. Well not this time! No opponent even touches Master Ip until the end fight with Japanese General Miura (Hiroyuki Ikeuchi). Even then, General Miura only gets in a few hits before Master Ip completely obliterates him, and I mean really, he friggin' puts that guy to

If there is ever a question about which is better as a close-quarters weapon, a gun or a martial artist, just refer to *Ip Man*. The answer is clear when a police officer is saying how this is the age of the gun, and martial artist Ip Man (Donnie Yen) renders said gun useless by dismantling it in seconds. Is that a bell ringing? Because that cop just got schooled by Master Ip!

In fact, there is a tremendous amount of schooling going on in *Ip Man*, both the teaching kind and the ass-kicking kind. Ip Man is the master of the martial art style Wing Chun, and quickly becomes known as the most skilled martial artist in Foshan after he wins a martial arts challenge against a highly skilled out-of-towner who is terrorizing the local martial arts schools. Things take a turn for the worst, though, when the Second Sino-Japanese War hits, and Ip and his family are forced into poverty under Japanese rule. Nobody can keep a good Ip Man down for long, though. After seeing several of his friends die unjustly, Ip Man gets mad! And then he gets really mad. And then the Japanese learn what it's like to be on the receiving end of an angry Ip Man, and they don't like him when he's angry.

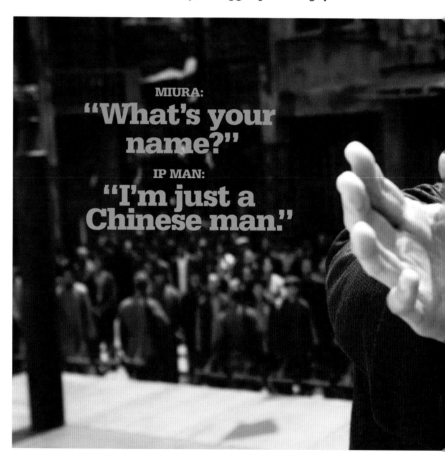

MIURA: **"What's your name?"**
IP MAN: **"I'm just a Chinese man."**

No-one likes Ip Man (Yen) when he's angry. Mandarin Films/The Kobal Collection

shame. With hands that move like thunder and feet that strike like lightning, one thing is clear: no one touches Ip Man; he touches you! And by touch, I mean knocks flat on your ass!

This film is a great one for action movie freaks because it combines an investing story with amazing martial art skills, and a little dash of history thrown in for good measure.

IN THE LAST GREAT WAR ONE MAN DEFIED AN EMPIRE...

DONNIE YEN

IP MAN

MENTOR OF ICONIC LEGEND
BRUCE LEE

Mandarin Films

Bloodsport

DIRECTED BY Newt Arnold
WRITTEN BY Menahem Golan (screenplay),
Christopher Cosby (screenplay), Mel
Friedman (screenplay), Sheldon Lettich
(screenplay and story)
STARRING Jean-Claude Van Damme,
Donald Gibb, Leah Ayres, Bolo Yeung
RELEASED Feb. 26, 1988
RATED R

A sure way to dodge the
grasp of a big bear man?
A splits-nutpunch combo.
Cannon/The Kobal Collection

You know what most movies are
missing? Guys doing the splits and
punching other guys in the crotch. Well
not *Bloodsport*! Loosely based on martial
artist Frank Dux's real life exploits, this
crotch-punching extravaganza stars Jean-
Claude Van Damme as Dux, a soldier
who goes AWOL in order to enter a
Hong Kong fighting tournament called the Kumite. This event is
known for being the most brutal, illegal, any-freakin'-thing-goes
quintessential martial arts fighting tournament this side of the
Mississippi. There are only three ways to win: "One, you knock the
guy right out; two, he shouts 'Mate.' It's like saying 'Uncle.' Three, you
throw the fucker right off the runway!"

Dux quickly makes friends with fellow American and martial
artist, Ray Jackson (Donald Gibb), who ends up playing the role of

JEAN-CLAUDE VAN DAMME

Bloodsport

FRANK DUX:

"Go for the gut. He's soft there."

Cannon

hypeman and best bud for Dux, making him the Richard Crenna of *Bloodsport*. And then they meet the real asshole of the tournament, Chong Li (Bolo Yeung), the returning Kumite champion famous for his thirst for blood and ruthlessness. He has maimed and even killed previous opponents just to win a match, and has such an overdeveloped chest that his rack would rival even Pamela Anderson's.

Dux and Li instantly become rivals and chomp at the bit to fight each other, so of course the final fight of the tournament comes down to Dux, "I'm a good hearted guy who plays fair," and Li, "I'd break my mamma's leg and leave her to a pack of wolves to win a fight."

This film has just the right amount of cheesy '80s stuff interspersed with awesome martial arts action. It comes fully equipped with spandex clothes, corny lines being delivered without even a hint of irony, and several training montages set to increasingly strange music. Oh, and tons of footage of JCVD doing the splits. He does them between two chairs, he does them with his hands and feet tied to some posts suspending him in air, he could and would split on a plane, he could and would split on a train!

Bloodsport also has a great display of many different styles of martial arts. This must have been a great flick for the stuntmen to work on because they each get a little time in the sun, showing off their fighting styles and actually getting to show their faces. And don't forget about Jean-Claude Van Damme! His skills are beyond impressive in this film, he's definitely riding high on the peak of his physical prowess. The guy's got punches for days, and helicopter kicks with enough power viewers will feel them from the couch!

As far as martial arts films go, *Bloodsport* can indubitably hold its own when compared to others. After all, it's about a fighting tournament! Films just don't get much more action centered than that.

Did you know *Mortal Kombat*'s Jonny Cage is based on *Bloodsport*'s Frank Dux? It's true! They both have the same propensity for wearing tight pants and doing crotch-punching splits.

Jean-Claude flexes his flexibility in a scene from *Black Eagle*. Rotecon/Magnus/Imperial Entertainment/The Kobal Collection

JEAN-CLAUDE VAN DAMME

"The muscles from Brussels," Jean-Claude Van Damme (JCVD), has two signature trademarks as an action star: doing the splits and 360-degree spin kicks. Oh, and maybe that he really likes showing off his butt.

JCVD is capable of pulling off these physically intense moves thanks to his background in kickboxing and karate, both of which he has trained in since he was a young child. He's an accomplished kick boxer, winning the European Middleweight Full-Contact Championship by knocking out his opponent in forty-six seconds and achieving a record of eighteen KOs. He continued to stack up more wins under his black belt but also took time out to study ballet, which probably helped him in doing the splits and increased his physical versatility, helping pave the way for him to become an action star.

He was given a small part in Chuck Norris's *Missing in Action*, and from there he went on to star in *Bloodsport*. Rumor has it that the original cut of the film was terrible, but JCVD helped edit it into shape and eventually convinced producers to release it. It's a good thing he did because that propelled him to stardom faster than a fart in a tornado. Some of his other most well-known pieces of work include *Double Impact*, *Hard Target*, *Timecop*, and *Universal Soldier*.

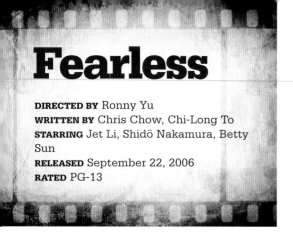

Fearless

DIRECTED BY Ronny Yu
WRITTEN BY Chris Chow, Chi-Long To
STARRING Jet Li, Shidō Nakamura, Betty Sun
RELEASED September 22, 2006
RATED PG-13

There are a lot of things that can induce fear. For some it's spiders, for others it's clowns, and for a select few, it's finding out *The Expendables 2* might be rated PG-13 instead of R. Every now and then, there are a few individuals who seem to be missing that fear button in their brain. *Fearless* is a film roughly based on the life of one of those fearless people, Chinese martial artist Huo Yuanjia.

They don't call Huo Yuanjia (Jet Li) fearless because he exhibits great bravery in the face of danger. Being brave indicates that the person is at least a little afraid of what he's facing to begin with, but does what he has to do anyway. Yuanjia is without fear, Daredevil style. Doesn't matter if he's facing one guy or twenty, Yuanjia goes into battle with the ice-cold demeanor of a substitute chemistry teacher.

Fearless takes place in 1910, a time when China's future was uncertain, and Westerners were more than happy to sweep in to exploit and humiliate them. Yuanjia steps up to restore China's pride by entering a fighting competition against a group of Westerners. Even though the battle is unfair, and the odds stacked high against him, Yuanjia goes in with confidence and honor, and immediately whips the asses of three of the four competitors. The film then flashes back to when Yuanjia is a child and follows his life story leading up to that fateful tournament.

Yuanjia experiences a wide character arc, beginning first as a cocky little bastard of a child/young man and growing into a humble, peaceful adult. The film illustrates the acting range and

HUO YUANJIA:
"Pussy claw?"

ZHAO JIAN:
"It's Tiger Claw!"

wushu skills of Jet Li, employing minimal wire-work in his fight scenes to give them a bit of added realism that his films normally lack.

Action freaks looking for more of a serious martial arts film can choose Fearless without fear that it will deliver a well-executed semi-autobiographical story and top-level action.

Huo locks blades with rival Master Chin. Beijing Film Studio/China Film Corporation/Hero China International/Wide River Investments/The Kobal Collection

JET LI IN HIS FINAL MARTIAL ARTS EPIC

JET LI'S
FEARLESS

A RONNY YU FILM

"Mastering others is strength. Mastering yourself makes you fearless." —LAO TZU

PG-13 PARENTS STRONGLY CAUTIONED
Violence and Martial Arts Action Throughout

From the producers of "HERO" and "CROUCHING TIGER, HIDDEN DRAGON"

www.jetlisfearless.com

ROGUE

Ninja Assassin

DIRECTED BY James McTeigue
WRITTEN BY Matthew Sand (screenplay/ story), J. Michael Straczynski (screenplay)
STARRING Rain, Rick Yune, Naomie Harris
RELEASED November 25, 2009
RATED R

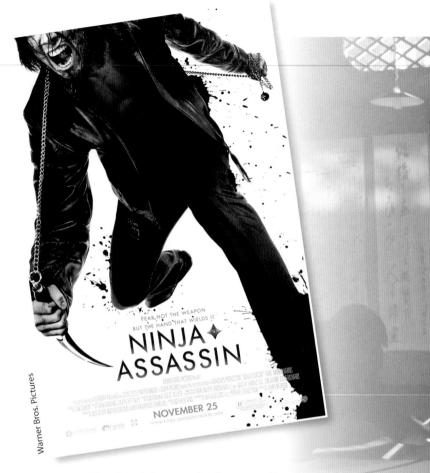

Warner Bros. Pictures

Here's a tip: if you ever receive an envelope full of black sand, RUN! However, it won't do you any good, because once that envelope is in your hands, it means the ninjas are already there, but at least you can die trying to get away.

Ninja Assassin is about ninja assassin Raizo, played by South Korean pop star Rain. Pop-star-turned-action star? Odd, yes, but he does a fine job in his performance, so don't worry. Anyway, as a child, Raizo was taken by Lord Ozuno (Sho Kosugi), head of the Ozunu clan, and raised as a member of the most lethal clan of assassins in the world. He becomes smitten with a girl also undergoing the ninja training and the two fall in love, which is a big freakin' no-no in his clan. She ends up executed for trying to escape, leaving Raizo feeling as pissed as a badger in a beehive.

Years later, Lord Ozuno tells Raizo to execute a different girl for trying to escape. When Raizo declines, Ozuno orders him executed instead, so Raizo flees and makes it his goal to save people

from being killed by the ninja assassin clan, as well as kill as many of them as possible, which makes him a ninja assassin assassin.

This film is a bloodbath of pure fun. Virtually every scene has someone getting beaten, stabbed, or decapitated, and always with a tsunami of blood gurgling out of every wound. Honestly, the sheer amount of CG blood spilled in this film is staggering. It's enough to keep a hundred vampires fed for a thousand years.

Though the plot and characterization both fall to the wayside in favor of the action, in this case I'd say it's for the better. *Ninja Assassin* features some of the coolest ninja-style action seen in modern cinema, with fights that often make fantastic use of the vast array of ninja weaponry, martial arts styles, and ninja skills so exceptional they border on magic. Honestly, most of the time the ninjas are doing magic—laws of reality be damned.

RAIZO:

"This is not my family. You are not my father. And the breath I take after I kill you will be the first breath of my life."

The back-flipping one-man army Raizo goes rogue on his former ninja clan. Warner Bros. Pictures/The Kobal Collection

Bangkok Knockout

DIRECTED BY Panna Rittikrai
WRITTEN BY Panna Rittikrai, Dojit Hongthong, Jonathan Simonoe
STARRING Gitabak Agohjit, Speedy Arnold, Supakson Chaimongkol
RELEASED Dec. 16, 2010 (Thailand)
RATED R

Fans of the *Ong-Bak* films, get ready for a 105-minute action extravaganza! Panna Rittikrai, the man behind *Ong-Bak*, *Born to Fight*, and *Chocolate*, as well as being Tony Jaa's mentor, is behind *Bangkok Knockout*. This time, instead of having one main character run around and kick ass, he puts his whole stunt team in the film, creating one crazy fun action film!

The story to *Bangkok Knockout* is about as basic as they come: after celebrating their victory at an athletic competition, a stunt team wakes up to find themselves trapped in a deadly game show where they have to fight to rescue one of their gal pals or die trying.

The story isn't done very well, and the acting is worse, but the action is absolutely fan-freakin'-tastic! There is 20 minutes of plot setup and poor attempts at humor, but then it gets to the good stuff and never stops. With approximately nine members of the stunt team all fighting their own battles, the film always has something exciting to throw at the audience, and the team members provide a wonderful visual variety with their mastery of different fighting styles, like Muay Thai and Capoeira.

Bangkok Knockout has a combination of brilliant stunt work, great locations for each action sequence, and wonderful use of props. For example, at one point, two guys are fighting in a cage where they jump, climb, and flip across the wire like spiders! Another scene pits our heroes up against a Thai Jason Voorhees look-alike armed with an axe, who manages to shrug off being lit on fire and repeatedly hit by a car. After a massive brawl between the many, many heroes and villains in the film, the lead protagonist and antagonist lock horns in a one-on-one fight during which

Members of a stunt team wake up to find they have two options: fight to rescue a friend or die trying. Na Film/Sahamongkolfilm/Magnolia Pictures

they're both hanging from the underside of a moving 18-wheeler! Most of these stunts were performed au naturel, without any sort of CG touch-ups, so every time it looks like these guys are risking life and limb, it's because they really are!

Another element that will appeal to the sensibilities of the modern action fan is the treatment of the female characters. Although both get kidnapped at some point, they do get in on the action and defend themselves, elevating them high above the status of "helpless female" seen so often in other films.

Na Film/Sahamongkolfilm/Magnolia Pictures

13 Assassins

DIRECTED BY Takashi Miike
WRITTEN BY Kaneo Ikegami (based on a screenplay by), Daisuke Tengan (screenplay)
STARRING Kôji Yakusho, Takayuki Yamada, Yûsuke Iseya
RELEASED Sept. 25, 2010 (Japan)
RATED R

If ever there was a dude you wouldn't want to antagonize, it would be a samurai, especially any of the samurai in the Japanese film *13 Assassins*. These guys could slice you like butter before the insult has left your filthy dog mouth! *13 Assassins* is a samurai epic loosely based on a true incident in which a Shogun's younger brother, Lord Naritsugu (Gorô Inagaki), becomes mad with power and goes around raping and murdering anyone that catches his eye, all without fear of reprieve due to his position. Eventually people get sick of Lord Naritsugu's nonsense and they hire Shinzaemon (Kôji Yakusho), a grizzled old samurai, to put an end to the cruelty. Shinzaemon recruits eleven other samurai and embarks on his near impossible mission to defeat Naritsugu and his army of 200.

Now, I know what you're thinking. Shinzaemon + eleven = twelve. Isn't the title of the movie *13 Assassins*? Why, yes it is. The thirteenth member of their merry band is Koyota (Yûsuke Iseya), a scruffy,

Shinzaemon (Yakusho), right, leads the mission to end a mad lord's cruelty.
Sedic/RPC/Dentsu/The Kobal Collection

役所広司
山田孝之　伊勢谷友
波岡一喜　近藤公園
吹石一恵　谷村美月
内野聖陽　光石 研
監督:三池崇史(「ク

146

命を、燃やせ。

13
十三人の刺客

www.13assassins.jp

Sedic/RPC/Dentsu

wild dog of a man they accidentally pick up in the woods. There are many solid performances throughout the film, but two that really stand out are Gorô Inagaki's portrayal of the bloodthirsty and thoroughly insane Lord Naritsugu, who is a villain so thoroughly detestable that by the end of the flick everyone will be screaming for his blood, and Yûsuke Iseya's fun, spirited performance as Koyota the wild man. *13 Assassins* is, for the most part, a dead serious film, and Koyota adds some much-needed levity to the affairs as well as providing a more "common-class" perspective to the rigidity of the samurai nobility, giving modern audiences a character to relate to.

This film is 141 minutes long and there's little in the way of action until the end; however, when it gets to the finale, the poop hits the fan and no one is safe from a big smelly splat. The end fight sequence is approximately forty-seven minutes of slicing, dicing, and explosions, resulting in blood-covered streets and multiple ponds made of two parts blood, one part water.

SHINZAEMON SHIMADA:

"No mercy! There's no samurai code or fair play in battle! No sword? Use a stick. No stick? Use a rock. No rock? Use your fists and feet! Lose your life, but make the enemy pay!"

Ong-Bak: The Thai Warrior

DIRECTED BY Prachya Pinkaew
WRITTEN BY Prachya Pinkaew (story),
Panna Rittikrai (story), Suphachai
Sittiaumponpan (screenplay)
STARRING Tony Jaa, Petchtai
Wongkamlao, Pumwaree Yodkamol
RELEASED January 21, 2003 (Thailand)
RATED R

With so many movies relying heavily on CG and special effects to bring in the audiences, it's good to know there are still guys out there willing to put their bodies on the line to deliver the most gritty, real performances possible. In *Ong-Bak*, leading man Tony Jaa does just that, giving a mind-blowing stunt fest that is 100 percent uncut Jaa. Accept no substitutions.

Ting (Jaa) is a peaceful man living in a small village in Thailand. That is, until the head of his village's beloved statue, Ong-Bak, gets stolen, leaving it up to Ting to get it back lest the village be cursed with draught and famine. One villager even goes so far as to tell him, "The fate of the whole village lies in your hands." Jeez! No pressure or anything. He should have added, "If you don't find the missing Ong-Bak head, we will just all die like dogs in the street. But hey, bring me back a Big Mac. I love those things!"

Jaa himself is a truly spectacular martial artist/stuntman, and *Ong-Bak* is an excellent demonstration of his abilities. With the wide variety of stunts he's capable of, they really manage to keep the film feeling fresh throughout, mixing up brutal Muay Thai brawls with death-defying stunts. For instance, at one point Ting is running from a group of thugs and during the chase, he jumps over cars, under cars, over tables, and best of all, through a barbed wire hoop so small, they'd be hard pressed to fit a twelve-pack of brewskis through it, let alone a person's whole body.

Action movie freaks must familiarize themselves with *Ong-Bak*. After the action gets started, it's non-stop knees and elbows to the faces of every bad guy who makes the mistake of crossing Ting, and stunt work so insane it'll make you pause the movie to say, "Did he really just do that?"

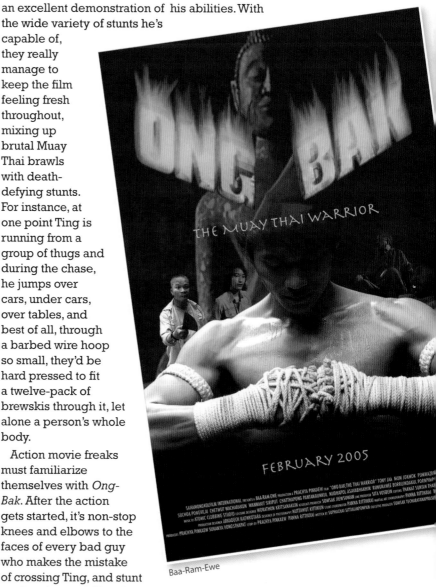

Baa-Ram-Ewe

BIG BEAR, A FIGHTER:
"Come on! Fuck Muay Thai!"

Tony Jaa's spectacular skills as a martial artist and stuntman take center stage in *Ong-Bak*. Baa-Ram-Ewe/The Kobal Collection

The Legend of Drunken Master

DIRECTED BY Chia-Liang Liu, Jackie Chan (uncredited)
WRITTEN BY Edward Tang (screenplay), Man-Ming Tong (screenplay), Gai Chi Yuen (screenplay)
STARRING Jackie Chan, Ho-Sung Pak, Lung Ti
RELEASED February 3, 1994 (Hong Kong)
RATED R

Sometimes a hero just needs a pick-me-up. Mario has his mushrooms, Popeye has spinach, and *The Legend of Drunken Master*'s Wong Fei-hung (Jackie Chan) has ... alcohol! As a master of Zui Quan, a.k.a Drunken Boxing, Wong gains strength with every swig of the intoxicating liquid, staggering around the battlefield like a toddler with a grudge to settle.

The sequel to the much more subdued *Drunken Master, The Legend of Drunken Master* concerns Wong's quest to stop the British consul from sneaking Chinese artifacts out of the country. Along the way, he accidentally destroys a building or two and gets temporarily disowned by his father. Good times!

This film is truly a must-see martial arts masterpiece, filled to the brim with jaw-dropping feats of physical exertion with some hit-

As usual, Jackie Chan doesn't disappoint with his jaw-dropping physical feats in *The Legend of Drunken Master*. Golden Harvest/Paragon/The Kobal Collection

or-miss comedy segments thrown in for good measure. Jackie Chan is someone known for combining humor and action, and this film is no exception. It's a light-hearted affair, with many of the battles containing his trademark use of props to keep the fisticuffs varied. And, Chan is definitely at his peak form. You may find bigger, more dangerous stunts in some of his other films, but here is where audiences see him at his fighting peak. He's ripped, limber, and pulling the kind of insane, often dangerous, martial arts antics that all little kids pretend they're doing when they're charging around the yard in their underwear and jump-kicking the air while screaming "Hi-YA!"

Though the film contains plenty of goodness throughout, it's the last third where it lives up to the name Legend. First, Wong faces off against China's notorious (and fictional) axe gang inside of a bar, battling an endless sea of hatchet-wielding cronies until the bar itself starts coming down. Then he faces off against the lead baddie inside a factory, and the two have a knock-down, drag-out brawl, during which Wong falls onto a sea of burning embers and has to crawl across it on his hands and feet, a stunt which Jackie Chan, as always, did himself. What a trooper!

In short, *The Legend of Drunken Master* is the kind of martial arts movie that every fan of face-punching, high-flying, ball-kicking movies should see.

Golden Harvest/Paragon/Heritage Auctions

JACKIE CHAN When it comes to stunt work, Jackie Chan is king. This loveable Hong Kong actor/stuntman has achieved worldwide fame through his prowess in acrobatics and martial arts, making him the go-to man for any action lover looking for enthralling, original stunts. Even if everything else about a film is crap, it's worth a watch at least once if it has stunt work by Chan.

In the United States, Chan is most well known for his work in *Rumble in the Bronx*, *Supercop*, *Drunken Master*, and *Rush Hour*, among several others. Not wanting to live in Bruce Lee's shadow, he set about creating his own brand of martial arts, incorporating humor and prop work into most of his stunts. Jackie Chan is a man known for taking anything around him and turning it into a weapon, including, but not limited to, jackets, tables, chairs, shopping carts, and lamps.

He started his training in singing, acrobatics, and martial arts at a young age, setting him up to become not only an accomplished stuntman, but a singer as well. Chan has spent most of his career performing his own stunts and expects the guys in his films to be able to do the same. Come on Jackie, not everyone can climb the side of a building like a squirrel or jump over a 15-foot gap. However, doing his own stunts has accomplished him two things in life. First, he holds the Guinness World Record for "Most Stunts by a Living Actor," and secondly, there isn't a company in the world that will insure the crazy bastard!

Performing stunts doesn't come without consequence, though. If a part of the body can be broken, Chan has probably broken it. Throughout his career, he's shattered his sternum, snapped his ankle, cracked most of his fingers, both cheekbones, and his nose, among other things. There was also one stunt that brought him within inches of death after he fell several feet, landed on his head and

suffered a skull fracture. Yet, here he is almost 60 and still making movies and doing stunts.

There is one thing Chan won't do, though, and that's sex scenes. He feels that the action people want to see him falling from a 60-foot clock tower or hanging onto a helicopter's rope ladder, not his between-the-sheets-style action.

Jackie Chan is definitely an icon, and has often been considered one of the most famous, if not the most famous, actor in the world. With a resume of more than 100 movies and no sign of slowing down, Chan's contribution to the world of action movies and movies in general is prolific, and something every action movie freak should take note of.

High-flying stunt work king Jackie Chan. Golden Harvest/The Kobal Collection

In 1940s Shanghai, China, a bumbling thief aspires to join a notorious gang in the zany and action-packed *Kung Fu Hustle*.
Columbia/Sony Pictures

SPECIAL SAUCE
Oddball Action

Sometimes people get in the mood for a little bit of a different flavor for their action movies, something other than the usual shoot 'em ups, car chases, or mano-y-mano brawl. It's the same as someone who has eaten that double patty cheeseburger with bacon and lettuce five days in a row—on day six they're looking to spice it up a bit by adding the "special sauce" to give that cheeseburger an extra oomph that's out of the ordinary.

In the action genre, most movies will play it safe and stick to the aforementioned car chases and shoot 'em ups, but there are other films, with bolder, more peculiar flavors, that sacrifice the conventional stylings in favor of breaking new ground. These oddball action films are the special sauce of the action genre—they combine the traditional ingredients in non-traditional ways (or sometimes forego ingredients all together) to do their own thing. People may have a hard time figuring out what's in it, and sometimes everything will just turn out to be a mess, but sometimes, when everything simmers *just* right, something truly special will come out of it.

So forget about trying to figure out oddball action movies and just enjoy. These bizarre films help keep the action genre from becoming stale with their quirky plots, offbeat action, and stylish cinematography.

Favorite *Evil Dead* series hero Ash (Bruce Campbell) is a triple-ass threat: badass, smartass, and dumbass, and he gets himself into more trouble in *Army of Darkness*. Dino De Laurentis

Oddball action can be about anything, like robot boxers fighting in the distant future or Chinese sorcerers duking it out in Chinatown. Or maybe it's not so much that they're strange per se, it's that they blend genres in an unusual way, such as the romantic-action-comedy *True Lies*.

While other movies might crack open the wall of realism, these flicks crash through it like the Kool-Aid Man, and all that can be said is, "OH YEAH!"

Big Trouble in Little China

DIRECTED BY John Carpenter
WRITTEN BY Gary Goldman, David Z. Weinstein, W.D. Richter (adaptation)
STARRING Kurt Russell, Kim Cattrall, Dennis Dun
RELEASED July 2, 1986
RATED PG-13

Big Trouble in Little China is an '80s classic and a perfect storm of bizarre special effects, an unusual story, and Kurt effin' Russell. Our boy Kurt stars as Jack Burton, a truck driver who finds himself in the middle of underground Chinatown fighting an ancient Chinese sorcerer, Lo Pan (James Hong). Burton is on a mission to get his stolen truck back from Lo Pan and help his friend, Wang Chi

Lo Pan's morning breath is not to be trifled with.
20th Century Fox/Heritage Auctions

On his mission to get his truck back, Jack Burton (Russell) accidentally does some heroic things. 20th Century Fox/Heritage Auctions

(Dennis Dun), save his girlfriend. Mostly, though, he just wants to get his dang truck.

This is a crazy movie that has to be paid attention to or else it won't make any sense. Hell, even if you do pay attention a lot of it won't make sense, but either way, it's still a fun ride from start to finish. Jack Burton is the clear fan-favorite character from *Big*

Normally everyone is safe when the hero shows up, but not necessarily so in Jack's case. 20th Century Fox/Heritage Auctions

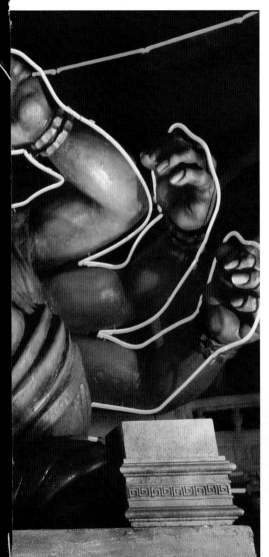

The movie has its share of solid fight scenes and shoot outs. 20th Century Fox/Heritage Auctions

Jack enlists the help of Egg Shen, a magician and authority on Lo Pan. 20th Century Fox/Heritage Auctions

"Everybody relax, I'm here."

Trouble in Little China. He's incompetent, selfish, not very bright, and as John Carpenter put it: "he's a hero who has so many faults. Jack is and isn't the hero. He falls on his ass as much as he comes through. This guy is a real blowhard. He's a lot of hot air, very self-assured, a screw-up." He's just the kind of non-traditional hero needed for an oddball film like *Big Trouble in Little China.*

Jack Burton's best quality, one that Mr. Carpenter forgot to mention, is his habit of accidentally taking himself out of the big fights by either knocking himself out or inadvertently throwing his knife across the room and then having to chase it down. And no matter what, his number one concern is always, "Where's my truck?" Oh, Jack, you silly bastard.

Big Trouble in Little China has the one-two punch of fun, original characters and over-the-top special-effects-laden action. Burton and Chi have a funny dynamic that keeps audiences laughing, and as a special bonus, there's a young Kim Cattrall, a.k.a that older gal from *Sex and the City.* Here she's youthful, beautiful, and most definitely not having any sex in the city.

The film benefits from having an original story centered around Chinese mysticism, sorcerers, beholders, and big, hairy, "what-in-the-hell-is-that-thing" monsters, all of which combine with the mighty directing power of John Carpenter and the mighty chin of Kurt Russell to make for one hell of a good time.

20th Century Fox/Heritage Auctions

KURT RUSSELL

There are few men with as much raw swagger as Kurt Russell. The man oozes confidence like some kind of confidence oozing beast from ancient times. And why shouldn't he? His acting accomplishments are a mile long, and his contributions to the world of action are staggering.

He began acting at a young age, starring opposite Will Hutchins in the pilot for the '50s' western *Sugarfoot*. From there, he had a variety of roles, everything from a jungle boy on *Gilligan's Island* to Elvis Presley in *Elvis,* which is when he joined forces with directing legend John Carpenter.

From there, the two collaborated on numerous occasions, creating some of cinema's most beloved cult classics, like *The Thing, Escape from New York/Los Angeles,* and *Big Trouble in Little China,* to name a few. Russell often plays anti-heroes, thanks in no small part to his handsome face, powerful physique, and a sneer that could melt the stink off of a zombie.

Kurt Russell as badass Snake Plissken.
Paramount/The Kobal Collection

The Good, the Bad, the Weird

DIRECTED BY Jee-woon Kim

WRITTEN BY Jee-woon Kim (screenplay), Min-suk Kim (screenplay)

STARRING Kang-ho Song, Byung-hun Lee, Woo-sung Jung

RELEASED July 17, 2008 (South Korea)

RATED R

Inspired by *The Good, the Bad, and the Ugly,* South Korean-made *The Good, the Bad, the Weird* is a diamond in the rough and an unadulterated oddball of an action film. This western's story is set in the 1930s and centers on three characters: the Good (Jung Woo-sung), a bounty hunter; the Bad, (Lee Byung-hun), an evil hitman; and the Weird (Song Kang-ho), a petty thief.

The Bad and the Weird are trying to steal the same treasure map being carried by a Japanese official on a train. The Weird ends up getting to the map first and makes off with it, with the Bad in hot pursuit. The Good, who happens to be on that same train, catches a glimpse of The Bad, a fugitive, and goes after him.

Sounds pretty wacky, right? Apparently that isn't wacky enough for writers Kim Jee-woon and Kim Min-suk because they throw

The Good (Woo-sung Jung) and the Weird (Kang-ho Song). Barunson/The Kobal Collection

the Japanese army and a gang of Manchurian bandits into the mix to create one bat shit loco movie! Throughout the film, the map is constantly being swapped around, changing hands more than *The Mexican's* eponymous pistol. It seems like everyone under the sun is willing to chase each other and gun down anyone in their way of this map that *might* lead them to treasure.

The Good, the Bad, the Weird is filled with high quality, complex action scenes throughout, with the finale being one of the high points of the film. In it, we have five parties altogether battling over the map, including an army on horseback chasing after an army in cars with mounted machines guns, and *those* men are chasing more men on horses chasing the Weird on a scooter! The Good and the Bad are mixed in there as well, but you'd be hard pressed to find them amidst all the gunfire, cannonballs, flails, exploding cars, and exploding people.

PARK CHANG-YI:

"People must know that they're going to die, and yet they live as though they never will. Hilarious."

Barunson

Crank/ Crank: High Voltage

DIRECTED/WRITTEN BY Mark Neveldine, Brian Taylor
PART 1: STARRING Jason Statham, Amy Smart, Efren Ramirez, Dwight Yoakam
RELEASED September 1, 2006
PART 2: STARRING Jason Statham, Amy Smart, Efren Ramirez, Clifton Collins, Jr.
RELEASED April 15, 2009
RATED R

Crank Series

Sometimes, when I get a little bored, I like to make up the most outrageous, nonsensical, eccentric action movie plots and imagine what the writer's room for that movie would be like.

Writer 1: Let's see ... let's make a film about a hitman who gets injected with snake venom by some rival enemies and the only way to stop the poison is to ... find the antidote?

Writer 2: No, too boring. Let's make the poison something rare and bizarre.

Writer 1: That's good, but we're still not there yet.

Writer 2: I agree. We have to up the ante somehow.

Writer 1: (snaps his fingers) I've got it! In order to stay alive, the guy who gets poisoned will have to keep his adrenaline pumping all the time to keep his heart from stopping until he can get the antidote.

Surrounded by men with itchy trigger fingers is no sweat for Chev Chelios (Statham).
Lionsgate Films/The Kobal Collection

Writer 2: Brilliant! That way, we can have him do all sorts of drugs, have sex in public, and crash cars while he gets revenge on the people who poisoned him. AND, because his adrenaline is pumping, we can have him fall out of a helicopter from thousands of feet up, crash onto a car, bounce off, and he will totally survive … because of the adrenaline! Then we can do a sequel once everyone figures out how awesome this movie is. We shall call this adrenaline junkie Chev Chelios and the ridiculous film shall be named *Crank*!

So I didn't actually come up with the above synopsis, but Brian Taylor and Mark Neveldine did, and it worked so well the first time around that they made a sequel. *Crank 2: High Voltage* follows the exact same path of wacky destruction only this time, Chev Chelios (Jason Statham) has his heart replaced with a battery-charged artificial one. Now, Chelios has to find his real heart, all the while finding ways to keep his artificial heart fully charged, even if that means electrocuting himself!

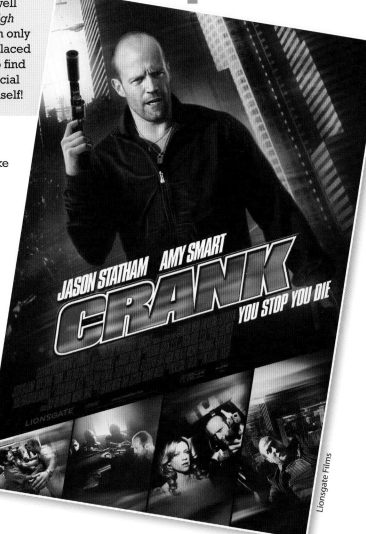

CHEV CHELIOS:
"Don't pop a blood vessel, you little penis."

JASON STATHAM   AMY SMART
CRANK
YOU STOP YOU DIE

LIONSGATE

Lionsgate Films

Crank is a very exciting, very, *very,* non-realistic, out-of-this-world-crazy-action-packed series; it's like a real-life version of the *Grand Theft Auto* games, only crazier. Between the two films, Chev Chelios flies high on drugs, gets into fights, drives cars through malls, shocks himself with jumper cables, gets electrocuted, and has a lot of sex in public. Like a *lot.*

Chelios is not the typical "hero" seen in action films. Actually, he's not really a hero at all. He's on a mission to save himself and that's it! Chelios isn't doing anything to save anyone else or better humanity. He's just a survivor and is hell-bent on getting revenge on the people who tried to kill him. However, on his road to vengeance, he pulls some amazing stunts and takes out some major criminal syndicates, making him kind of a hero as well as a total badass.

Crank houses one of the "manliest" kills I've ever seen, hands down. Chelios is driving a car with his girlfriend, Eve (Amy Smart), in the passenger seat, and they are trying to escape from the bad guys. Chelios' adrenaline starts to wane, so Eve decides to help out by laying her head in his lap and performing a ... favor of sorts. While this is going on, the baddies come up beside their car. Chelios shoots out the passenger side window without looking, hits the driver, and the car crashes—all the while getting pleasured by his pretty lady.

With that kind of craziness, people would think they couldn't top it with a sequel—and they'd be wrong. *Crank: High Voltage* is one of those sequels that hits harder and explodes bigger, but these films are so bizarre that they are best suited in the oddball action section. The sequel's filled with more kills, more boobs, and more outrageous, implausible plot. Really, if you like a movie that has a deeper message and meaningful plot, then see this flick anyway and learn to appreciate the madness.

The *Crank* series is a must-watch set for action movie freaks. Don't watch it with anyone you'd be embarrassed to watch a porno with, though, as the films are pretty sexually charged. And, just like a porno, they're full of action and the plot doesn't matter.

CHEV CHELIOS:

"Who's got my fucking strawberry tart?"

Jump-start my heart: Chev needs to find ways to keep his artificial heart fully charged, even if it means electrocuting himself. Lionsgate Films/The Kobal Collection

The athletically talented Jason Statham in a scene from *Transporter 2.* Europacorp/TFI Corp/The Kobal Collection

JASON STATHAM

Jason Statham hit the ground running with his film debut in 1998 with *Lock, Stock and Two Smoking Barrels,* and ever since then he's been stuck in high gear, starring in multiple action films per year. Since 1998, he has landed roles in more than 30 films. He made such a name for himself, he was given the privilege of being part of *The Expendables,* which houses the biggest action stars from the '80s to today, starring as Lee Christmas, Barney Ross' (Sylvester Stallone) right-hand man and the film's deuteragonist.

Statham's prowess in martial arts, diving, and acrobatic maneuvers allows him to perform most of his own stunts. He's a true man of action, not just an onscreen one. He studies kickboxing, Wing Chun, kung fu, and karate, has been diving since he was a wee lad, finishing 12th in the World Championships in 1992, and was also a member of Britain's National Diving Squad for 12 years, so there's no wondering why he makes an excellent action star. His British accent and rugged good looks don't hurt him, either.

His first lead role was in *The Transporter,* which went on to have two sequels. He also stars in the insane series *Crank.* In both 2011 and 2012, Statham starred in four, count 'em, *four,* movies. Before then, he's had at least one film every year if not two or three. And these films are high quality action films, too, not just cheesy crap thrown on a screen … except maybe for Uwe Boll's *In the Name of the King: A Dungeon Siege Tale.* Even stars like Statham are in the occasional stinker.

A hard-working man of few words and lots of kicks, Jason Statham has definitely earned his stripes as an action star. Anyone looking for a lot of action can look no further than his vast and rapidly expanding library of film roles.

Army of Darkness

DIRECTED BY Sam Raimi
WRITTEN BY Sam Raimi, Ivan Raimi
STARRING Bruce Campbell, Embeth Davidtz, Marcus Gilbert
RELEASED February 19, 1993
RATED R

Hail to the king, baby! Bruce Campbell is back as Ash Williams, everyone's favorite borderline-dickhead hero, in *Army of Darkness,* also known as *Bruce Campbell vs. Army of Darkness,* the third installment of the horror series *Evil Dead*. One of this film's classifications may be horror, but it's not scary at all. What it is, though, is filled with one of the strangest bits of action and comedy seen outside of '80s anime.

At the start of the film, Ash has been sucked through a time portal and is now in 1300 AD. At first he's captured by Lord Arthur and his men and cast into a pit containing Deadites, the *Evil Dead*'s brand of undead creatures. Ash proves himself to be a mighty warrior (and more than a little unhinged) by slicing/blowing the nasty beasts to bits with his chainsaw/shotgun combo.

Lord Arthur and his men accept him as one of their own, and beseech him to retrieve the Necronomicon, a book of dark magic that will stop the attacks from the undead, as well as return Ash to his native time. Ash agrees and journeys to find the book, along the way encountering his evil self, a book that sucks him into another

dimension, and skeleton hands that poke him in the eyes *Three Stooges*-style. When Ash forgets the magic words he is supposed to say when retrieving the Necronomicon and just *coughs* the last word of the phrase, all hell breaks loose and an army of darkness, lead by Evil Ash, comes hunting for the living.

Perhaps the most enduring thing about the *Evil Dead* series is Ash himself. Played to utter perfection by Bruce "If Chins Could Kill" Campbell, Ash manages to simultaneously be a badass, a smartass,

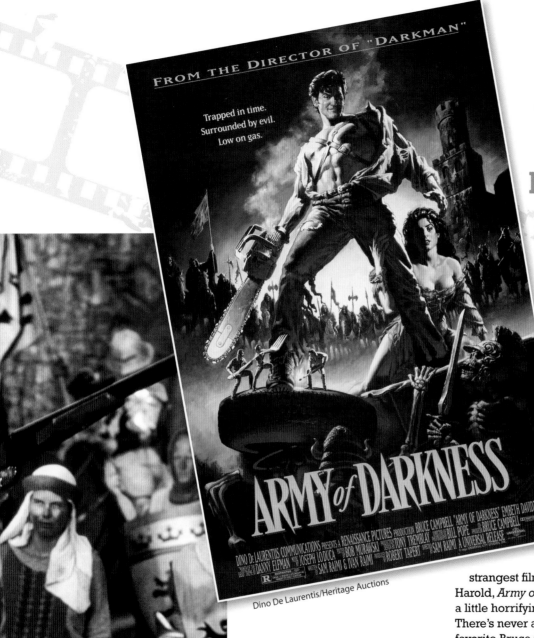

FROM THE DIRECTOR OF "DARKMAN"

Trapped in time.
Surrounded by evil.
Low on gas.

ARMY of DARKNESS

DINO DE LAURENTIIS COMMUNICATIONS PRESENTS A RENAISSANCE PICTURES PRODUCTION BRUCE CAMPBELL "ARMY OF DARKNESS" EMBETH DAVIDTZ
MUSIC BY DANNY ELFMAN AND JOSEPH LODUCA DIRECTOR OF PHOTOGRAPHY BILL POPE PRODUCED BY BRUCE CAMPBELL
EDITED BY BOB MURAWSKI ASSOCIATE PRODUCER TONY TREMBLAY EXECUTIVE PRODUCER ROBERT TAPERT WRITTEN BY SAM RAIMI & IVAN RAIMI DIRECTED BY SAM RAIMI A UNIVERSAL RELEASE

Dino De Laurentis/Heritage Auctions

Ash and his trusty boomstick.
Dino De Laurentis/The Kobal Collection

ARTHUR:
"Are all men from the future loud-mouthed braggarts?"

ASH:
"Nope. Just me baby ... Just me."

and a dumbass. Nearly every line out of his mouth is quotable perfection, from "Groovy" to "THIS IS MY BOOMSTICK!" There's a reason that people are still quoting the guy two decades later.

Overall, *Army of Darkness* stands as one of Hollywood's strangest films. Much like weird cousin Harold, *Army of Darkness* is strange, funny, a little horrifying but always entertaining. There's never a dull moment, and with fan-favorite Bruce Campbell leading the way as Ash, the king of snark himself, action fans are in for one hell of a time.

The Boondock Saints

DIRECTED/WRITTEN BY Troy Duffy
STARRING Sean Patrick Flanery, Norman Reedus, Willem Dafoe
RELEASED Jan. 21, 1999
RATED R

Have you ever wondered what the Green Goblin would look like as a woman? Neither have I, but *The Boondock Saints* answers this unasked question by flinging Willem Dafoe in drag into viewers' faces like a monkey flinging poo. In addition to cross dressing, he's frenching dudes! But that's not all *The Boondock Saints* is about, there's also the MacManus twins (Sean Patrick Flanery and Norman Reedus), a.k.a the Boondock Saints, who are on a holy mission after receiving a message from God while in jail. That message went a little something like this: "Go dispense some good old-fashioned street justice on the criminals of Boston, and do it with great haste, and make sure to say a cool prayer whenever you kill one of them. Those prayers are totally boss."

The Boondock Saints is anything but a typical action movie. The criminals are chatty and occasionally friendly (right before they bash someone's face in), the heroes are two good Catholic boys, and even the action itself is presented

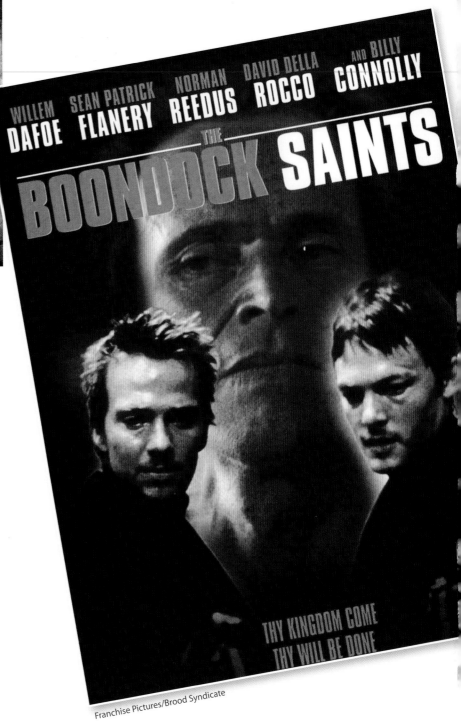

Franchise Pictures/Brood Syndicate

unusually. For example, often a scene will begin with a pile of dead bodies, and Willem Dafoe, using his master forensic detective skills, will walk us through the action scene in reverse, showing each step taken and shot fired by the Boondock Saints.

The inspiration for *The Boondock Saints* came from writer/director Troy Duffy's disgust at seeing a drug dealer stealing money from a dead guy and turning that disgust into a screenplay about two brothers cleaning up the criminal element. Hey, looks like every cloud does have a silver lining!

Despite a limited theatrical run, *The Boondock Saints* has a very loyal, very *large* cult following, enough so that a sequel was made, *Boondock Saints II: All Saint's Day.* The sequel continues the story of the MacManus twins and mixes up the formula with the addition of the brilliant and beautiful federal agent Eunice (Julie Benz). It seems that the MacManus brothers have a certain charm that appeal to people. Maybe it's because they're Irish, or maybe it's because they go around mowing down bad guys without mercy, for no reason of their own! They aren't out for revenge, no one killed their parents when they were children or burned their house down or anything. Nope. All it takes is one message from God to light a fire under their tushies and send them out the door to scrub the criminal scum right off the streets.

CONNOR:

"Do ya know what we need, man? Some rope."

MURPHY:

"Absolutely. What are ya, insane?"

CONNOR:

"No I ain't. Charlie Bronson's always got rope."

Murphy (Reedus) and Connor (Flanery) clean up the criminal element in their town with some old-fashioned street justice. Franchise Pictures/Brood Syndicate/The Kobal Collection

The Fifth Element

DIRECTED BY Luc Besson
WRITTEN BY Luc Besson (story/
screenplay), Robert Mark Kamen
(screenplay)
STARRING Bruce Willis, Milla Jovovich,
Gary Oldman
RELEASED May 9, 1997
RATED PG-13

One would think a film in which the main hero and villain never meet, never talk to each other, and aren't even aware of each other might not work out very well, but it does in *The Fifth Element.*

The hero, Korben Dallas (Bruce Willis), and one of the villains, Zorg (Gary Oldman), never cross paths throughout the entire movie. Action movie freaks' brains are programmed by all the other films that a villain and a hero must know about and *must* fight each other or else the movie has no purpose. But *The Fifth Element* saw this standard and said "No sir!" and in doing so helped forge an unconventional classic.

Villain Zorg (Oldman) never meets his nemesis Korben. Columbia/Tri-Star

Korben Dallas (Willis) finds himself at the center of a battle to save humanity. Columbia/Tri-Star/The Kobal Collection

"I hate warriors. Too narrow-minded. I'll tell you what I do like though: a killer, a dyed-in-the-wool killer. Cold blooded, clean, methodical, and thorough."

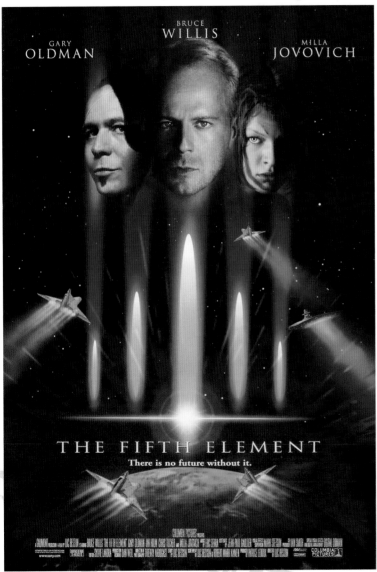

Columbia/Tri-Star

Set in 23rd century New York City, cab driver Korben Dallas is minding his own business when a passenger drops in. Literally, in this case, as she crashes through the roof. Korben finds out that his unexpected passenger, Leeloo (Milla Jovovich), is the human embodiment of the Fifth Element, a sacred aspect of the universe whose job it is to combine the power of the four classic elements, earth, water, fire, and air, into the Divine Light in order to battle The Great Evil, which is a giant malevolent black fireball. With Korben leading the way, Leeloo and her group (indirectly) battle Zorg in a race to collect the five elements.

The Fifth Element features a wide array of fantastically memorable characters. Bruce Willis has the easy job portraying a sort of Space John McClane, while Jovovich plays Leeloo with both a childlike innocence and overwhelming sense of power, and Chris Tucker rounds out the trio as a fast-talking, egomaniacal talk show host.

The film features a universe full of bizarre aliens and mechanized weirdoes, and thanks to the exceptional creature effects, they still retain their brand of unique charm rather than going the route of CG creatures of the time and aging worse than a Bel-Air housewife. Though the action might sometimes take a backseat to the weirdness of the universe and characters, there's still plenty of it. In fact, one of the film's indoor explosions was the biggest ever filmed at that time, and the resulting fire nearly burned down the studio. When a film almost destroys the studio due to the insane special effects, it means they're doing something right.

Milla Jovovich in her breakthrough role as Leeloo. Columbia/Tri-Star

When action freaks hear "Leeloo Dallas Mul-ti-pass," they think of the beautiful Milla Jovovich in *The Fifth Element*. In this breakthrough role, Milla managed to bring a strong duality to the character of Leeloo, seeming both powerful and vulnerable, comedic and stern, knowledgeable and naive all at once. From there, she's had a lengthy career of shooting zombies and snapping necks on the big screen. She portrayed the character Alice in *Resident Evil* with such ferociousness that it spawned four more sequels (as of this writing, anyway. With the way the *Resident Evil* movie franchise is going, they won't stop making them until Milla's decided she's sick of kicking zombies in the head). In the first *Resident Evil*, she performed almost all of her own stunts, wanting to put the kickboxing, karate, and combat training she'd received to good use. She's also notoriously bad at pulling her punches, something that resulted in more than a few black eyes for the unlucky undead actors in her flicks.

Strangely enough, Jovovich has also had a lengthy career as a model, giving her the odd role of being a woman both beautiful enough to look glamorous and strong enough to look like she could pile drive some zombie ass. Her modeling career began early, at the age of nine, and since then she has been on the cover of more than 100 magazines. She speaks Serbian, English, and French fluently, and, as if all that isn't enough, she's also a critically acclaimed singer and songwriter. Good grief, Milla, leave something for the rest of the world to be good at!

One person's dream world is another person's nightmare. In the future world of *Demolition Man*, there is absolutely no crime, every restaurant has been bought out by Taco Bell and turned into one, and there's no stinking toilet paper. Whether this sounds like heaven or hell depends on a person's priorities, but I'd rather risk getting mugged once in a while than have to wipe using three seashells.

Demolition Man presents a quirky and satirical version of 2032, a world in which cursing is a "crime" worthy of getting a fine for and even kissing and sexual relations are forbidden. These things present problems only for Sergeant John Spartan (Sylvester Stallone) and violent criminal Simon Phoenix (Wesley Snipes), seeing as how they were both cryogenically frozen in the year 1996 and have been revived in 2032 to find themselves in a strange new world.

Demolition Man

DIRECTED BY Marco Brambilla
WRITTEN BY Peter M. Lenkov (story/screenplay), Robert Reneau (story/screenplay), Daniel Waters (screenplay)
STARRING Sylvester Stallone, Wesley Snipes, Sandra Bullock
RELEASED October 8, 1993
RATED R

Romance blossoms between police partners John Spartan (Stallone) and Lenia Huxley (Bullock).
Warner Bros./Silver Pictures/The Kobal Collection

SIMON PHOENIX:
"Simon says, Die."

In 1996, Spartan arrested Phoenix for his various crimes, but not before Phoenix could frame Spartan for the killing of 30 hostages, which lands both of them in jail and subsequent cryogenic suspension. When Phoenix is unfrozen for a hearing, he escapes, and since the police aren't used to handling such ruffians, they resuscitate Spartan so he can do their dirty work.

Demolition Man represents an offbeat take on the action genre, deriving much of its humor from Spartan being such a fish out of water. The casting is spot-on, with Stallone bringing his standard strong-jawed charm to the role of John Spartan, and Sandra Bullock performing admirably as Lenia Huxley, Spartan's progressive-minded partner in the future. Wesley Snipes, however, really shines in his role. His athleticism is unparalleled here-the man's punches and kicks were so fast, in fact, that he had to slow them down in order for them to be filmed properly-and he plays Simon Phoenix with a sort of psychotic glee, making him the kind of villain people love to hate. He and Stallone have great verbal, as well as physical, sparring, tossing out more cheesy lines than a pick-up artist looking to score.

Those looking for something old and something new in an action movie can look no further than *Demolition Man,* with its blend of a traditional action movie wrapped up in a nontraditional future city.

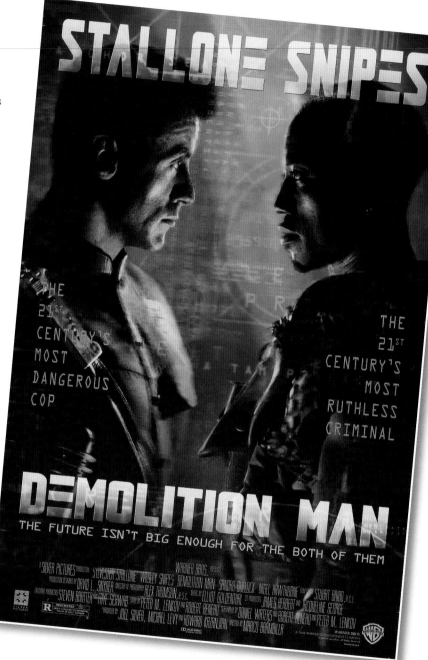

Warner Bros./Silver Pictures

Great Onscreen Fights Between Famous Actors

Action movies are often famous for their one-on-one throwdowns, and sometimes these epic duels have helped propel the actors to stardom; other times they're fan-service battles between everyone's favorite thespians.

Here is a list of some well-known actors and actresses and the films famous for their furious fisticuffs.

FILM	FIGHT BETWEEN
BATMAN BEGINS	Christian Bale and Liam Neeson
BLOODSPORT	JCVD and Bolo Yeung
DEMOLITION MAN	Wesley Snipes and Sylvester Stallone
THE EXPENDABLES	Jet Li and Dolph Lundgren
THE EXPENDABLES	Sylvester Stallone and Steve Austin
FACE/OFF	John Travolta and Nicholas Cage
FAST FIVE	Vin Diesel and Dwayne Johnson
THE FORBIDDEN KINGDOM	Jackie Chan and Jet Li
KILL BILL VOL. 1	Uma Thurman and Lucy Lui

Sylvester Stallone and Wesley Snipes are just two of many famous actors and actresses who have fought onscreen. Here they're in a scene from *Demolition Man* as John Spartan and Simon Phoenix, respectively. Warner Bros./Silver Pictures/The Kobal Collection

Great Onscreen Fights Between Famous Actors

FILM	FIGHT BETWEEN
KILL BILL VOL. 2	Uma Thurman and David Carradine
LETHAL WEAPON	Mel Gibson and Gary Busey
LETHAL WEAPON 4	Mel Gibson and Jet Li
LIVE FREE OR DIE HARD	Bruce Willis and Maggie Q
LONE WOLF McQUADE	Chuck Norris and David Carradine
MR. & MRS. SMITH	Angelina Jolie and Brad Pitt
THE ONE and WAR	Jet Li and Jason Statham
ROCKY I & II	Sylvester Stallone and Carl Weathers

FILM	FIGHT BETWEEN
ROCKY IV	Sylvester Stallone and Dolph Lundgren
THEY LIVE	"Rowdy" Roddy Piper and Keith David
UNDER SIEGE	Steven Seagal and Tommy Lee Jones
UNIVERSAL SOLDIER	Jean-Claude Van Damme and Dolph Lundgren
WAY OF THE DRAGON	Chuck Norris and Bruce Lee

Uma Thurman and Lucy Liu clash swords in *Kill Bill.* A Band Apart/Miramax

Jet Li unleashes some fury in a scene from *Unleashed*. Rogue Pictures/The Kobal Collection

JET LI

Jet Li became a notable wushu martial artist at a young age, beginning his training at eight years old and retiring at only seventeen. Some people don't even get started "living life" until they're seventeen, but Li had already won fifteen gold medals and one silver in Chinese wushu championships. Where does a person go from there? To star in action films, naturally.

He made his debut appearance in *The Shaolin Temple,* starting a Kung fu boom in China, and then relocated to Hong Kong, furthering his success by appearing in over forty films and counting, including his distinguished work in *Once Upon a Time in China*. It wasn't long before Jet Li's talent was noticed overseas, and he began making Hollywood blockbusters like *Lethal Weapon 4, Hero, Kiss of the Dragon, The One,* and *The Forbidden Kingdom,* ultimately leading to his spot as one of the powerhouse performers in *The Expendables*.

True Lies

DIRECTED BY James Cameron
WRITTEN BY James Cameron (screenplay),
Claude Zidi (screenplay- La Totale!),
Simon Michaël (screenplay- La Totale!),
Didier Kaminka (screenplay- La Totale!)
STARRING Arnold Schwarzenegger, Jamie
Lee Curtis, Tom Arnold
RELEASED July 15, 1994
RATED PG-13

Harry is a classic '90s action hero. Lightstorm/20th Century Fox/Heritage Auctions

You know *True Lies* is going to be awesome when the start of the film is Arnold Schwarzenegger in a tuxedo being asked to see his invitation, to which Arnold responds, "Sure, here's my invitation," before blowing something up. Thank you, James Cameron.

In *True Lies*, Arnold plays Harry, an undercover spy. To his family, though, he's just a traveling salesman who spends too much time on the road, something that leaves his wife, Helen (Jamie Lee Curtis), feeling neglected and bored, ultimately leading her into some shenanigans of her own.

After a lengthy series of *Three's Company*-esque rom-com situations, Helen and Harry are taken hostage by a madman looking to detonate a nuclear bomb. During said kidnapping, Helen sees that Harry has been keeping some of his special skills from her, like his ability to snap a guy's neck like a twig or his intricate knowledge of terrorist behaviors, which leaves Harry with some 'splaining to do!

In sickness and in undercover spying: Harry comes clean with wife Helen about his real identify. Lightstorm/20th Century Fox/Heritage Auctions

There are so many wonderful things about *True Lies*. For starters, it's directed by James Cameron. Oh, no big deal, he's just the guy who's behind several films in this book, including Terminator 2 and Aliens, not to mention the many other excellent non-action films on his resume. The man knows how to handle an action scene and adds style and value to whatever he does.

Great director? Check! Great cast? Check check! *True Lies* stars Arnold Schwarzenegger, Jamie Lee Curtis, and Tom Arnold, each of whom bring their own style of humor to the flick. There's even Bill "Game Over Man, Game Over" Paxton and a young Eliza Dushku for everyone's viewing enjoyment. But wait! There's more! The rugged Charlton Heston and sexy Tia Carrere also grace the screen with their talent.

True Lies is the best example of the Bro Code being executed to perfection, as Gibson (Tom Arnold) is the kind of bro that every person needs. He's constantly covering for Harry with his wife. He is there for Harry when they think Helen is cheating on him, he goes along with Harry when he wants to kidnap the guy he thinks is his wife's male mistress (what do you call that? His wife's mister?

Her maestro?). Gibson is also willing to sign some papers and/or knock out a guy when Harry is stealing a fighter plane. Overall, the man's bro-hood is exemplary, in both the spy world and the real world, and he deserves "The Best Bro of the Year Award." He's Arnold's MVB.

Action wise, *True Lies* definitely won't disappoint. It's a perfect example of '90s action movies, filled with Arnold one-liners, constant explosions, and so many dead henchmen you'd need an abacus to keep track of them all. And Arnold's character is the classic '90s action hero, an invincible spy so ultra-awesome he doesn't even get out of breath or break a sweat. That's professionalism, people.

So why is *True Lies* an oddball action flick? Because it's two parts action movie sandwiched around one part romantic comedy, putting it in the barely existent category of true romantic-action-comedy movies.

When he said I do,
he never said
what he did.

Schwarzenegger
True Lies

A JAMES CAMERON FILM

TWENTIETH CENTURY FOX PRESENTS A LIGHTSTORM ENTERTAINMENT PRODUCTION A JAMES CAMERON FILM ARNOLD SCHWARZENEGGER TRUE LIES JAMIE LEE CURTIS TOM ARNOLD BILL PAXTON ART MALIK TIA CARRERE ELIZA DUSHKU MUSIC BRAD FIEDEL EDITED BY MARK GOLDBLATT, A.C.E. CONRAD BUFF AND RICHARD A. HARRIS PRODUCTION DESIGNER PETER LAMONT DIRECTOR OF PHOTOGRAPHY RUSSELL CARPENTER SPECIAL VISUAL EFFECTS DIGITAL DOMAIN EXECUTIVE PRODUCERS RAE SANCHINI ROBERT SHRIVER LAWRENCE KASANOFF SCREENPLAY BY JAMES CAMERON AND RANDALL FRAKES STORY BY JAMES CAMERON BASED ON THE FILM "LA TOTALE!" BY CLAUDE ZIDI, SIMON MICHAEL AND DIDIER KAMINKA

OPENS JULY 15   PRODUCED BY JAMES CAMERON AND STEPHANIE AUSTIN DIRECTED BY JAMES CAMERON

HELEN TASKER:

"Have you ever killed anyone?"

HARRY:

"Yeah, but they were all bad."

Gibson (Arnold) is exemplary in his execution of the Bro Code for Harry. Lightstorm/20th Century Fox/Heritage Auctions

Kung Fu Hustle

DIRECTED BY Stephen Chow
WRITTEN BY Stephen Chow, Huo Xin, Chan Man-keung, Tsang Kan-cheung
STARRING Stephen Chow, Wah Yuen, Qiu Yuen
RELEASED December 23, 2004 (international)
RATED R

"How did I get in this barrel? Does anybody know?" If you find yourself asking this question, chances are you've just faced off against Sing (Stephen Chow) or another Kung fu genius, and you're trapped inside the movie *Kung Fu Hustle*. If you find that to be the case, may I suggest you either 1. Start practicing your ass-kicking skills, or 2. Start practicing your ass-kissing skills.

Shanghai in the 1940s is overrun with gangs, the fiercest of them all being the Axe Gang, named for their weapon of choice. One quaint little village named Pig Sty Alley accidentally provokes the Axe Gang, and the villains attack the helpless people and ... totally get their asses kicked! Surprise! The village houses some of the most powerful "retired" martial artists in China, who promptly send the Axe Gang home with tails tucked between their legs.

Embarrassed about getting their butts handed to them in a paper cup, the Axe Gang sets out to get revenge on the poverty stricken village. After their hired assassins kill several of Pig Sty Alley's supreme Kung fu masters, a wannabe Axe Gang member, Sing, finds himself conflicted. He's always wanted to join the Axe Gang, but was never deemed talented enough. Now that he's facing their bullying behaviors, he finds that his long-dormant sense of justice is bubbling up, and in turn, awakening his equally dormant skills as a Kung fu genius. Just in time, too, as now he finds himself facing off against the entire Axe Gang and the monstrous Kung fu master, The Beast!

Kung Fu Hustle is overflowing with cartoonish, over-the-top action, with Sonic the Hedgehog-like running sequences and fist prints

Sing (Chow) hustles some foes. Columbia/Sony Pictures/The Kobal Collection

indenting the faces of countless goons. Overall, the fights climb right up the wall of reality and then topple off, Humpty-Dumpty style, into a realm devoid of the grim seriousness typical of many martial arts flicks. The film makes great use of CGI and wirework, and director/star Stephen Chow employs slow-motion wisely to help the audience enjoy every outlandish detail.

The cast is truly top-notch as well. Stephen Chow brings likeability to Sing, a lead character who is, for about ninety percent of the movie, an ill-mannered dickhead. In addition to Chow, martial arts aficionados will be excited to see the faces of some of their favorite actors from '70s Kung fu movies, as Chow sought out some of the greatest martial arts actors of yesteryear, like Yuen Qiu as the sarcastic Landlady, Yuen Wah as her subservient husband, Bruce Leung, who was Stephen Chow's childhood hero, as the grotesque Beast, and cameos from Zhang Yibai and Feng Xiaogang as Inspector Chang and the leader of the Crocodile Gang, respectively.

Kung Fu Hustle is a cross between a martial arts epic and Looney Toons, and it's the perfect choice for an action movie freak looking for something a little different in their martial arts comedies.

The Landlady (Yuen Qiu) has a little more going on behind those curlers and chain-smoking persona.
Columbia/Sony Pictures

LANDLADY:
"You may know Kung fu... but you're still a fairy."

Sci-Fi Action Movies

Even though science fiction movies are just that, fiction, they still often have elements of plausibility to them. While things like zombies don't exist, per se, watching movies about them will make you wonder: could they? DUM DUM DUM!

While most action movies try to stay at least somewhat realistic, sci-fi action movies have no such limitations. All the writers have to do is set up the rules for the story and they can just go nuts, really letting any and every idea they have come forth for our viewing entertainment. Any kind of technology can exist. If a character needs a wristwatch that can make pancakes in mid air to avoid starvation, all a writer has to do is put it down on paper and it's pancake time.

With science fiction, viewers can see anything from super computers to all-purpose sonic screwdrivers, lecherous androids, and laser guns with British accents—the combinations are endless. And when that same formula is taken and applied to action movies, it results in genetically enhanced heroes running through the wreckage of New York City, rebounding up walls, and gunning down mega werewolves, all so they can deliver water to the last city on Earth.

So if the action classics are the meat and bun, martial arts are the lettuce, and oddball films are the special sauce, then sci-fi action movies are the french fries. Much like french fries, sci-fi action movies are different than their contemporaries

and bring their own original, but much needed flavor, to the table. And many of the greatest action movies have science fiction elements to them—*The Terminator* series, *RoboCop*, *Total Recall*—all films enhanced by the addition of these fantastical elements.

All in all, science-fiction action movies are versatile, multi-genre films, so suit up and ready your mind for a journey through an infinite sea of possibilities.

Total Recall has it all: a prime Arnold Schwarzenegger, cheesy one-liners, mutants, and three-boobed hookers. Carolco/Heritage Auctions

Predator

DIRECTED BY John McTiernan
WRITTEN BY Jim Thomas, John Thomas
STARRING Arnold Schwarzenegger, Carl Weathers, Kevin Peter Hall
RELEASED June 12, 1987
RATED R

A predator is any organism that lives by preying on others, i.e. by killing and/or eating it. Here's a fun fact: in the wild, predatory animals don't always kill their prey prior to feeding on them, so that's a pleasant thought! Humans have always been at the top of the food chain, but that's all about to change in *Predator*.

The Predator. 20th Century Fox

A special forces team of seven is dropped into the Guatemalan jungle under the impression they're saving a presidential cabinet member from a team of guerilla forces. On the way to the guerrilla camp, they stumble across some corpses with their skin ripped off, which some might find odd, but they stay on task and attack the camp, killing everyone but one woman that they take hostage.

During the team's hike through the jungle, something malevolent watches from afar. When the team members start getting killed by this invisible, unknown creature, they have to think fast and figure out how to catch something they can't see. It seems like the predators … have become the prey.

Most of *Predator* is classic Schwarzenegger work. He delivers the one-liners, kicks ass, fights a ludicrously powerful foe, and he's one of the few people to walk out alive.

DUTCH: "If it bleeds, we can kill it."

Dutch and his team try to figure out who or what is hunting them. 20th Century Fox/Heritage Auctions

Speaking of his foe, holy crap is Kevin "Predator" Peter Hall a giant. At seven feet two inches, the man is a titanic terror, towering over Schwarzenegger in every scene. Another element that ups his scariness level is the incredible creature effects at work on the Predator himself: the suit, the weapons, the creepy animatronic face beneath the creepy mask. All of it blends together to create an unforgettable villain, one who is motivated only by the most primal of villainous motivations—the kill.

This film is a veritable who's-who of athletes-turned-actors-turned-elected-officials, with both Schwarzenegger and professional wrestler Jesse "The Body" Ventura having been

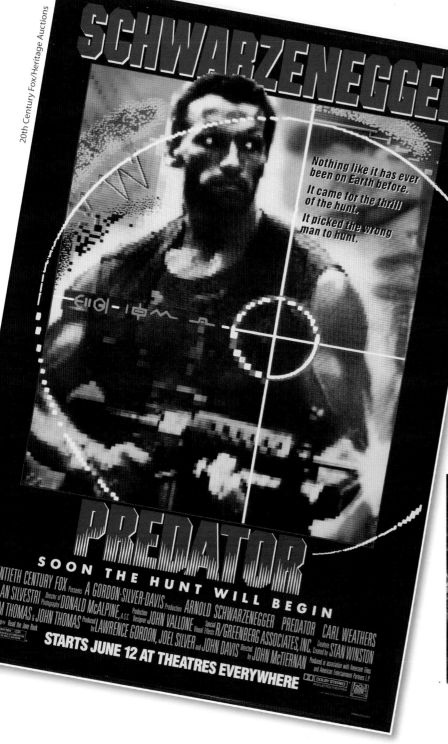

SCHWARZENEGGER

Nothing like it has ever been on Earth before.

It came for the thrill of the hunt.

It picked the wrong man to hunt.

PREDATOR

SOON THE HUNT WILL BEGIN

TWENTIETH CENTURY FOX Presents A GORDON·SILVER·DAVIS Production ARNOLD SCHWARZENEGGER PREDATOR CARL WEATHERS
ALAN SILVESTRI Director of Photography DONALD McALPINE, A.S.C. Production Designer JOHN VALLONE Creature Created by STAN WINSTON Visual Effects R/GREENBERG ASSOCIATES, INC.
JIM THOMAS & JOHN THOMAS Produced by LAWRENCE GORDON, JOEL SILVER and JOHN DAVIS Directed by JOHN McTIERNAN Produced in association with Amercent Films and American Entertainment Partners L.P

STARTS JUNE 12 AT THEATRES EVERYWHERE

elected to public office. Now if only we could get Carl Weathers elected governor of Wyoming, we'd really be cooking.

Predator is definitely a hybrid film, balancing action, sci-fi, and horror together to create something entirely new. Despite the rampant amount of manliness and ass-kicking at the beginning of the film, there's always this pervasive feeling that something really bad is lurking in the shadows, just waiting to maim and dismember any lambs who stray too far from the herd.

As a horror movie, the film is intense, filled with pulse-pounding action, brutal gore, and an ever-rising kill count. As an action movie, it stands above the rest, with Arnold's team of super soldiers and the awesome one-liners from the man himself. If you see the movie playing anywhere, do yourself a favor and "steek around."

Only one man has what it takes to take down the beast.
20th Century Fox/Heritage Auctions

185

RoboCop

DIRECTED BY Paul Verhoeven
WRITTEN BY Edward Neumeier, Michael Miner
STARRING Peter Weller, Nancy Allen, Dan O'Herlihy, Kurtwood Smith
RELEASED July 17, 1987
RATED R

RoboCop is here to serve and protect … unless someone is breaking the law, in which case he's here to stomp and dismember.

When police officer Alex Murphy (Peter Weller) is killed while busting a gang for robbery, his department takes the most logical next step: they turn him into a cyborg named RoboCop. After this transformation, RoboCop goes out on the streets and starts cleaning up the trash, throwing baddie after baddie in the slammer. Things are fine until the day he comes face to face with one of his killers from his human life, and he starts to feel a little … confused. Memories of his human life come pouring in and he doesn't know what the hell's going on until Anne Lewis (Nancy Allen), the

RoboCop renders a weapon useless. ITV Global/Heritage Auctions

RoboCop's partner when he was human, Anne (Allen), helps him remember the man inside the machine. ITV Global/Heritage Auctions/Deana Newcomb

"Dead or alive, you're coming with me!"

woefully inept cop who was his partner when he got gunned down, figures it out and helps RoboCop remember the man inside the machine.

RoboCop is very much a commentary on American society in the '80s, filled to the brim with corrupt businessmen whose only concern is the bottom dollar, as well as fake news segments interspersed with advertisements for children's board games about global nuclear destruction. Seems like people had a pretty bleak outlook on the future circa 1987.

RoboCop has had a lasting legacy in both the science fiction and action genres. The American Film Institute placed *RoboCop* on two of its top film lists including "Top Ten Science Fiction Films" and "Top 100 Thrills," as well as *Entertainment Weekly* placing it as the 14th greatest action movie of all time. It has been nominated for several Academy Awards, winning one for sound effects editing.

As an action movie somewhat slower than modern films, what action it does have is piled high with savagery and gore, and the combination of '80s satire and the struggle to find humanity in an increasingly mechanized society are two things that have helped give *RoboCop* such long-lasting popularity.

RoboCop takes to the streets to start cleaning up the trash. ITV Global/Heritage Auctions/Deana Newcomb

Total Recall

DIRECTED BY Paul Verhoeven
WRITTEN BY Philip K. Dick (short story, "We Can Remember It For You Wholesale," inspiration), Ronald Shusett (screen story/screenplay), Dan O'Bannon (screen story/screenplay), Jon Povill (screen story), Gary Goldman (screenplay)
STARRING Arnold Schwarzenegger, Sharon Stone, Michael Ironside
RELEASED June 1, 1990
RATED R

Ever feel like getting away from it all? Of course you do. Why not take a vacation by swimming in the ocean blue, or riding the world's tallest rollercoaster? Better yet, why not "get your ass to Mars" with Arnold Schwarzenegger in *Total Recall*!

This film depicts a future where humanity has colonized many different planets, and most people spend their hard-earned coin on virtual vacations—implanted memories of a vacation without the muss or fuss of actual travel. When Quaid (Schwarzenegger) decides to take a virtual trip to Mars, it's discovered that he's already had a memory wipe ... which means something is amiss. He wakes before the vacation can even begin, and he's confused, angry, and getting attacked by everyone he ever knew, including his sweet wife, Lori (Sharon Stone).

Quaid then receives a message from his pre-memory-wipe self telling him that he used to work for the Mars administrator killing rebels, decided to quit, and his ex-employer must be the reason why he had his memory wiped. So Quaid takes an actual trip to Mars to get to the bottom of things and find out who he really is. The real question is, however, is this all happening for real, or is it just implanted memories!?!

This sci-fi classic delights in messing with the minds of both Arnold and the viewers alike—you'll go cross-eyed trying to keep track of who's good, who's bad, who needs saving, and who should be left out in the uncontrolled Mars atmosphere to die of asphyxiation. Even poor Benny (Mel Johnson, Jr.), the funny cab driver, switches sides so many times he doesn't know which way he's looking until he is staring at the business end of an oversized drill Quaid is pushing toward him, muscles flexing as he screams, "Screw youuuuuu!!!" Everything becomes (more or less) clear in the end, but until then the film takes the viewer on a little joy ride of "Guess who's going to screw over Quaid next?"

There's never a dull moment in *Total Recall* between the twisting plot, the dynamite action, the mesmerizing mutants living on the Mars colony, and Arnold makes more strange Arnold faces than you can shake a three-breasted hooker at.

Total Recall **messes with the minds of Arnold and viewers alike.** Carolco/Heritage Auctions

Lori and Doug share a loving embrace shortly before their unorthodox divorce. Carolco/Heritage Auctions

The hooker brigade. Carolco/Heritage Auctions

Quaid may not know who he is, but he does know how to fight. Carolco/Heritage Auctions

SCHWARZENEGGER

Get ready for the ride of your life.

TOTAL RECALL

LORI:

"Doug, honey ... you wouldn't hurt me, would you, sweetheart? Sweetheart, be reasonable. After all, we're married!"

DOUGLAS QUAID (after shooting Lori in the head, killing her):

"Consider that a divorce!"

ARNOLD SCHWARZENEGGER

He's been a terminator, a barbarian, a cop multiple times over, a Greek god, and even Danny Devito's twin brother, and he is none other than Arnold Schwarzenegger! Let's face it: Arnold has been a huge influence on the world of action movies. Known for being in movies with over-the-top action, Arnold is a master of delivering priceless one liners all while having a chiseled hard rock body making him look sexy/threatening. He could be holding twelve puppies licking his face and the baddies would still run from him thanks to the superhuman amount of swagger in his every step.

Starting off as a body builder gave Arnold the awe-inspiring physique that added to his credibility as an action star. Few actors had those kinds of muscles in action films at the time, and in stepped Arnold to give the "action hero" a new look. He holds the record for youngest person to win the Mr. Olympia competition at the age of 23, and went on to win the competition six times in a row before retiring to give the other guys a chance. However, while training for his role in *Conan the Barbarian*, he got back into such good shape, he decided he wanted to win Mr. Olympia one more time, which he did in 1980. Mix that kind of athletic stature with his signature Austria accent and you've got one hell of an action star!

Arnold was voted the 53rd "Greatest Movie Star of all Time" by *Entertainment Weekly*, and, well, it's probably not for his acting skills seeing as how he's been nominated for a Razzie Award for Worst Actor eight times. Nonetheless, he makes up for his lack of acting range by playing basically one character, and playing him really well.

Most films Arnold has starred in have become timeless classics and favorites for action movie freaks, films such as *Conan the Barbarian*, the *Terminator* series, *Commando*, *The Running Man*, and *Predator*. Action movie freaks can thank Arnold for hours and hours of golden entertainment. I mean—the man's name is synonymous with "action star," and if it weren't for him, the world of action movies would be very different than it is today. It'd be crappier.

Arnold Schwarzenegger in all his physical glory playing the title role in *Conan the Barbarian*. De Laurentis/The Kobal Collection

Aliens

DIRECTED BY James Cameron
WRITTEN BY James Cameron (story and characters), David Giler (story), Walter Hill (story), Dan O'Bannon (characters), Ronald Shusett (characters)
STARRING Sigourney Weaver, Michael Biehn, Carrie Henn, Lance Henrikson
RELEASED July 18, 1986
RATED R

At the heart of the movie is the bond between Ripley and Newt.
20th Century Fox/Heritage Auctions

The team examines some facehuggers. 20th Century Fox/Heritage Auctions

There's a reason that Ellen Ripley (Sigourney Weaver) is one of the most famous heroines in cinema history. It's because while everyone around her is shaking in their boots, she picks up a gun and starts kicking some alien ass!

Ripley is found (fifty-seven years after the events of Alien) at the beginning of the movie drifting around in space in hypersleep. As soon as she's woken up, everyone around her scoffs at her story of an alien attacking her ship and killing everyone onboard. FOOLS!

Eventually, contact is lost with a colony of space settlers … a colony that was built where Ripley and crew first encountered the alien eggs. Despite repeated warnings from Ripley, a team of marines is formed to go check out the situation, dragging her along on the agreement that any aliens, egg or otherwise, are to be killed on sight. They go to the colony and find that everyone is fine, and that their communication systems went down because of a power surge. Then Ripley and her team hang out and celebrate

Christmas, and Ripley learns the true meaning of the holiday. By the way, that's totally not what happens. There's no one at the colony because some freakin' aliens killed them all! "Game over man, game over!"

While *Alien* was more focused on being a sci-fi horror film, its sequel, *Aliens*, adds a third ingredient to the brew: action. It also brings greater depth to the character of Ripley, giving the audience a close view of the pain she feels from having missed fifty-seven years of her life, as well as her struggle for her voice to be heard in a world more focused on profits than human life. It's a superior science fiction film chock full of suspense, mixed with action, and even a little bit of humor at times, not to mention what everyone wants in a movie: really big guns!

When people think of action heroines, Ripley is usually the first place their mind goes to, and for good reason. Like *Terminator*'s Sarah Connor, she's a

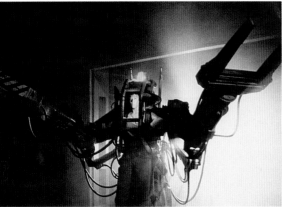

Ripley suits up to take on the queen alien "bitch."
20th Century Fox/Heritage Auctions

20th Century Fox/Heritage Auctions

The aliens like to smile before spitting their powerful saliva in people's faces.
20th Century Fox/Heritage Auctions

Between aliens and terminators, the '80s were a rough time for Michael Biehn. 20th Century Fox/Heritage Auctions

RIPLEY:

"These people are here to protect you. They're soldiers."

NEWT:

"It won't make any difference."

survivor who has to fight not only against the monsters trying to kill her, but the people trying to silence her stories of what's really going on. Not to mention that, back in the time period when *Aliens* came out, there were few women in serious action roles, and when Ripley was introduced as a respectable, smart woman who can handle a weapon and did the rescuing instead of being the "girl in distress," it really hit the mark with audiences.

Aliens also has some of the best creature effects in cinema history. Even by today's standards, the aliens look both awe-inspiring and terrifying, all thanks to the terrific practical effects used to create them.

Action movie freaks will love the great story, incredible suspense, phenomenally action-packed finale, and the outstanding ass-kicking heroine. Throw in creature effects that will give you nightmares for years to come, and you've got yourself one hell of a movie!

Underworld: Awakening

DIRECTED BY Måns Mårland, Björn Stein
WRITTEN BY Len Wiseman (screenplay/
story/characters), John Hlavin
(screenplay), J. Michael Straczynski
(screenplay), Allison Burnett
(screenplay), Kevin Grevioux
(characters), Danny McBride (characters)
STARRING Kate Beckinsale, Michael Ealy,
India Eisley
RELEASED January 20, 2012
RATED R

Vampires, werewolves, and a sexy lady with an icy gaze and enough cold-blooded ruthlessness to keep an entire meat locker frozen are the kinds of things *Underworld: Awakening* has to offer. Before vampires and werewolves became the pansies they are in Twilight, they were vicious beasts known for chowing down on humans when they weren't too busy killing each other in their centuries-old war.

In *Underworld: Awakening*, Kate Beckinsale reprises her role as the vampire Selene. In this fourth installment of the *Underworld* series, the humans have discovered that vampires and Lycans exist and freaked out about it, causing a mass persecution of the "diseased." Selene and her hybrid lover from the first two films, Michael, end up captured by the humans and cryogenically frozen to be used as research subjects for a "cure."

Fast forward twelve years later, Selene finds herself unfrozen by a mysterious benefactor. After killing a crap ton of guards, she escapes the lab and goes in search of Michael, but finds instead that she has a twelve-year-old hybrid daughter, Eve (India Eisley), who was the one that helped her escape.

Eve is a hot commodity to the Lycans, just like her daddy was in the first film, and the evil Dr. Lang (Stephen Rea) plans to use her blood to perfect the Lycan race, 'roiding them out to make them bigger, stronger, and immune to silver. He's already started the experiment on his son, producing an Ultra Mega Lycan! (Note: that's not their official name.)

This film starts off with bullets-a-blazing and hardly slows down to take a breath! The few breaths it does take are just to spit out a sentence or two of exposition before the bullets start flying again. Even though it has the least amount of plot, the fights are the most vicious, gory, and the most fun of the series. If more character development is what someone is looking for, the best choice would be to watch the original *Underworld*, which balances out the action and characterization with a bit more finesse. For those searching for an action only, "plot is for babies" type of film, *Underworld: Awakening* will hit the spot.

SELENE:
"My heart is not cold. It's broken."

Selene's vampire ally David (Theo James) rallies other vampires to fight a possible human attack.
Screen Gems/The Kobal Collection

5 Hell on Heels

KATE BECKINSALE

Kate Beckinsale might not be the first person thought of when talking about amazing action actresses, but she's easily a contender. Her mad action skills are so amazing that I think I've got a little bit of a girl crush on her.

She has played many characters of great strength, both physical and emotional, and perhaps none is better known than Selene, the death-dealing vampire from the *Underworld* series. Selene is a character draped in coolness. She's determined, unafraid, and maybe a little cold hearted, but hey, she's a friggin' vampire, so I guess we can let her slide on that last one. She is a trained Death Dealer, which is vampire-ese for someone who kills the crap out of anyone giving her vampire coven any grief.

Beckinsale also plays tough-gal Anna Valerious from *Van Helsing* who, like Selene, learns to protect herself at a young age, and again, like Selene, spends all of her time dealing with vampires and werewolves. Beckinsale practically has a PhD in werewolf slaying after *Van Helsing* and three *Underworld* films. She pulls off the role of the action heroine with ease and grace, making her one of the top action females of Hollywood.

Kate Beckinsale as the vampire Selene.
Subterranean/Screen Gems/The Kobal Collection/Egon Endrenyi

Dawn of the Dead

DIRECTED BY Zack Snyder
WRITTEN BY George A. Romero (1978 screenplay), James Gunn (screenplay)
STARRING Sarah Polley, Ving Rhames, Mekhi Phifer
RELEASED March 19, 2004
RATED R

A film that encompasses multiple genres, and my personal favorite zombie flick, Zack Snyder's 2004 remake of George Romero's *Dawn of the Dead* is a great mix of action, horror, and science fiction elements, all combining together to create a film so good each genre wants to claim it as its own.

"It's horror!"

"No, you idiot, it's sci-fi!"

"You're both wrong, it's an action movie!"

Well, whatever kind of film it is, it definitely goes for broke with scenes of action so huge and intense the audience will need a mouth guard so they don't bite their lips off and a seatbelt so they don't fall off the edge of their seats.

Ana (Sarah Polley) is a hospital nurse; she's a sensible gal with a good life and a loving husband. But after a shift at the hospital filled with patients bearing infected bite wounds, things start to get out of hand. The next morning, she wakes up to find that things aren't just out of hand— someone's bitten the whole hand off!

The entire city has become overrun

Ana (Polley) and Kenneth (Rhames) find themselves surrounded by fast flesheaters.
Strike Entertainment/New Amsterdam/The Kobal Collection/Michael Gibson

TERRY:

"Bart, dude, everybody's dead, okay? Your mom's dead. Your brother's dead. That fat chick at Dairy Queen? Dead!"

with zombies trying to chow down on anyone not in their elite club. Confused as to what's happening, Ana's survival instincts kick in and she gets the heck out of dodge, only to end up crashing her car. Eventually she and a few other survivors decide to hole up in a mall until they can be rescued. So they wait … and wait … and realize that rescue may not be coming. The group has to make the best of a bad situation inside this shopping mall, all the while making sure that the hordes of flesh-eating zombies don't find their way inside.

There are so many factors that make this film wonderful, with the first, and perhaps most influential, being the introduction of running zombies. Previously zombies were creatures known for their slow, deliberate pace. The remake, however, decides to hell with that and makes those suckers sprint like road runners with bottle rockets strapped to their butts. After seeing hordes of decrepit corpses running after the characters, it will be hard to find the old school, slow zombies all that scary anymore.

WHEN THERE'S NO MORE ROOM IN HELL
THE DEAD WILL WALK THE EARTH

DAWN OF THE DEAD

UNIVERSAL PICTURES PRESENTS A STRIKE ENTERTAINMENT/NEW AMSTERDAM ENTERTAINMENT PRODUCTION "DAWN OF THE DEAD" SARAH POLLEY VING RHAMES JAKE WEBER AND MEKHI PHIFER
MUSIC BY TYLER BATES SUPERVISED G. MARIO BOSWELL EDITED BY NIVEN HOWIE PRODUCED BY ANDREW WICKODOWANY PHOTOGRAPHY BY MATTHEW F. LEONETTI ASC CO-EXECUTIVE THOMAS A. BLISS DENNIS E. JONES ABRAHAM BERNSTEIN
www.dawnofthedeadmovie.net PRODUCED BY RICHARD P. RUBINSTEIN MARC ABRAHAM ERIC NEWMAN BASED ON SCREENPLAY BY GEORGE A. ROMERO SCREENPLAY BY JAMES GUNN DIRECTED BY ZACK SNYDER
STRIKE [THIS FLICK IS NOT YET RATED] A UNIVERSAL PICTURE

COMING SOON

Dawn of the Dead features other top-notch elements like kick-ass heroine Ana, who keeps her cool in the most difficult situations (see Best Narrow Escape, P. 198), and Ving Rhames doing what he does best: being a total badass. The film is an almost non-stop barrage of terror and gore, with exploding heads a-plenty. With this perfect blend of action, sci-fi, and horror, *Dawn of the Dead* is sure to appease fans of all three genres.

Best Narrow Escape:
Dawn of the Dead

This prize would have to go to Ana (Sarah Polley) for having to fight off her beloved zombie husband. Here's what happens:

The zombie outbreak has just begun to spread when Ana and her hubby wake up and see their neighbor, a young girl, standing in the hallway with blood on her face and nightgown. Not thinking anything of it, the husband goes to see if he can help her when suddenly she bites a huge chunk out of his throat. Ana pulls the little girl off her husband and pushes her down the hall, quickly slamming and locking the door before trying to help her husband. She's barely had enough time to dial 911 when hubby dearest kicks the bucket thanks to his massive blood loss.

Don't cry, though, because he's not dead for long. Soon he's up and running again, only this time it's as a bloodthirsty zombie looking to make himself a zombie wife. Seeing this, Ana dives into the bathroom, slams the door shut, and falls into the tub. After a few seconds of tense silence, her zombie husband starts breaking down the door, and she narrowly manages to make it outside and into her car.

But it doesn't stop there! The undead madman runs outside and leaps onto the car, getting one good punch into the windshield before falling off as she drives away. Whew! What an escape!

Ana frantically tries to escape her bloodthirsty zombie husband.
Strike Entertainment/New Amsterdam

Serenity

DIRECTED/WRITTEN BY Joss Whedon
STARRING Nathan Fillion, Gina Torres, Summer Glau, Chiwetel Ejiofor
RELEASED September 30, 2005
RATED PG-13

FOX may have cancelled the popular television show *Firefly* after only airing eleven of the fourteen episodes, but they should've known that they couldn't stop the signal. Joss Whedon, creator and writer of the show, persevered and continued the sci-fi space adventure through the film *Serenity*.

In the distant future, overcrowding on Earth has forced humans to move out to other star systems and take up residence there. River Tam (Summer Glau) is a mentally ill psychic who spent years in an Alliance government laboratory, undergoing torturous experimental procedures. Her brother eventually finds and frees her, and the two end up on the firefly-class starship Serenity, captained by the roguish Malcolm "Mal" Reynolds (Nathan Fillion). The Alliance, fearing that River knows the truth behind the dirtiest of their dirty secrets, dispatches The Operative (Chiwetel Ejiofor) and assigns him with one task: kill River Tam. On top of all this, there's also the Reavers, monstrous, disfigured humans who've spent the last decade terrorizing border colonies and ravaging their people.

Serenity, like much of Joss Whedon's work, is a complex tale with conflicts and characters who are far from black and white. The Operative, an ice-hearted bastard who will murder children if he believes it will help him succeed in his mission to keep the peace for all of the citizens of the Alliance, isn't your typical villain, and Mal isn't your typical hero, as he's constantly forced to choose ignobility if it

Capt. Mal Reynolds (Fillion), center, and his Serenity crew.
Universal Studios/The Kobal Collection/Sidney Baldwin

The Matrix

DIRECTED BY Andy Wachowski, Lana Wachowski

WRITTEN BY Andy Wachowski, Lana Wachowski

STARRING Keanu Reeves, Laurence Fishburne, Carrie-Anne Moss, Hugo Weaving, Joey Pantoliano

RELEASED March 31, 1999

RATED R

Laurence Fishburne excels in the role of Morpheus. Warner Bros./Heritage Auctions

There is one blue pill and one red pill before you. If you take the blue one, you will go on with life as usual; however, if you take the red one, your eyes will be opened to the reality of action movies! I cannot promise that it will be easy ... once your eyes have been opened, an addiction to action movies is bound to occur. Which pill do you take? In *The Matrix*, Neo (Keanu Reeves) chooses the red pill, opening his eyes to a little more than he bargained for.

The film follows a group of people fighting to free humanity from overly intelligent machines. In the real world, the machines have enslaved mankind in fluid-filled pods, like little babies in a womb, harvesting body heat to use it for energy. To keep the enslaved people docile and harvest-able, the machines have created the Matrix, a computer generated artificial reality based on life in the late '90s.

A group of rebels have managed to free themselves from the Matrix, with one of them being Neo. He is thought to be "the one" who will end the war against the machines. Neo (an anagram for One, gasp! Clever points!) embarks on a journey to master the matrix, overcome the machine empire, and free humanity. No biggie.

The Matrix's name is synonymous with action movies. It received many Oscars as well as a Saturn Award for Best Science Fiction film and was named ABC's fourth best sci-fi film by popular vote. It's also one of the few action movies that can't, in good conscience, be accused of having no plot. In fact, the first half or so of the film drags ever-so-slightly under the weight of the incredible amount of background information they have to cover. It's well worth it, however, as the plot is a tripped out, mind-boggling ride, blending

NEO:

"What is the Matrix?"

TRINITY:

"The answer is out there, Neo, and it's looking for you, and it will find you if you want it to."

Trinity (Moss) mesmerizes a cop with her ability to defy gravity before delivering a demolishing kick. Warner Bros./Heritage Auctions

Neo (Reeves) squares off against nemesis Agent Smith (Weaving). Warner Bros./Heritage Auctions

beginner's philosophy with modern sensibilities about the independence of man from their machines. It really makes you think … not for long, though. Once the plot's been established, the action kicks up exponentially, ending with Neo and Trinity (Carrie-Anne Moss) demolishing pretty much everything that moves!

Acting isn't always Keanu Reeves' strong suit, which is weird, since, you know, it's his job, but he does a decent enough job here. Carrie-Anne Moss does well with little to work with, given that Trinity is about as personable as a dentist's chair. Laurence Fishburne and Hugo Weaving, however, really excel as Morpheus and Agent Smith, respectively. Fishburne brings a sense of belief to even the most convoluted of dialogue, and Weaving's Agent Smith is one of film's greatest villains. He's a computer program with an aberrant hatred of humanity, and Weaving has all the right moves, facial tics, and vocal inflections to really make Agent Smith so much more than a well-dressed bad guy.

The visual effects and fight choreography were revolutionary for its time and left a lasting influence on the way action movies are made. Since *The Matrix*, action films have begun employing "bullet time," where a character slows down or freezes, but the camera moves around giving the audience a good look at what action is happening.

Watching *The Matrix* can be symbolic of a coming of age for any action movie freak, as it will open your eyes to what, exactly, it means to be an action movie. So do you watch *The Matrix*, or not!?! Red pill or blue?

THE TOY

Superhero and Video Game Action Films

Superpowers! Oh how awesome it would be if people did have superpowers. And by people, I mean me, because I would use mine for good, not evil. Unless someone was being a douche and pissed me off, in which case, I'd punch them into New Jersey.

Regardless, there's a little part of everyone that wishes they had a superpower, that they, too, were one of the *special* ones. And

Angelina Jolie brings video game adventurer Lara Croft to life in *Lara Croft: Tomb Raider.* Lawrence Gordon/Mutual Film/Paramount/Heritage Auctions/Alex Bailey

since we can't live in a world with people like that, we, instead, create worlds for audiences to enjoy.

Likewise, video games allow us to get to live vicariously through someone else with fantastic powers or living in a fantastic world. Given that the player is too busy experiencing the story to often pay much attention to it, video games haven't always had the most complex of tales woven within them, which makes them perfect for adapting into an action movie!

Video game movies and superhero movies are often shallow, shiny affairs, and that's the way I like 'em. But they're also stories about heroes facing overwhelming odds to do what's right, which is the core sentiment behind every great action movie. They're glitzy, they're sparkly, and if you stare at them too long, you may start to notice all the little flaws. They're like the toy at the end of our hamburger meal—something shiny and fun that'll keep our excitement up long after the meal is finished.

The Dark Knight

DIRECTED BY Christopher Nolan
WRITTEN BY Jonathan Nolan (screenplay),
Christopher Nolan (screenplay/story),
David S. Goyer (story), Bob Kane
(characters)
STARRING Christian Bale, Heath Ledger,
Aaron Eckhart, Gary Oldman, Michael
Caine, Maggie Gyllenhall, Morgan
Freeman
RELEASED July 18, 2008
RATED PG-13

If Batman has time to prepare, you are going to lose. It doesn't matter who you are, what sort of powers, skills, or resources you have, you are going to freaking lose. Why? Because he's the God-damned Batman, that's why! In *The Dark Knight,* we have English Batman up against Australian Joker, as Christian Bale and Heath Ledger face off in Christopher Nolan's tour de force of a film.

The Dark Knight is the second of a three-part series directed by Nolan. Bruce Wayne, a.k.a Batman (Bale), has been on the scene for a while now, raining down on Gotham's criminal element like a monsoon. But he worries that his crusade for justice will consume his life; that it will never end. When district attorney Harvey Dent (Aaron Eckhart) comes along, Bruce Wayne realizes that the hardworking idealist may be the hero that Gotham needs, and that maybe he can finally hang up his cowl. But before he can get too comfortable with that idea, the Joker shows up, people start dying, and things start getting blown up. A *lot.*

The Dark Knight has achieved incredible financial and critical success thanks to its excellent writing, incredible stunt choreography, and bold acting. The action itself varies widely with Batman knocking out people using the brutal Keysi Fighting Method, and the Joker wreaking sheer havoc, causing lengthy car chases, numerous explosions, and making a pencil disappear. Each of *The Dark Knight's* action sequences propels the story forward, managing to be both exciting as an action sequence and enriching for the characters.

Outside of the action, you have an endless list of fantastic performances. Christian Bale brings the kind of strength and torment that's needed to play Batman, Gary Oldman's Commissioner Gordon is the last good cop left in Gotham, and Oldman portrays the Commish with relatability. Michael Caine is, of course, awesome as Alfred, Bruce Wayne's butler/confidante/father figure, and he nicely balances sage advice with a bit of Cockney humor. Eckhart has one of the toughest jobs of the cast, as Harvey Dent has arguable the widest character arc of the film, first earning our belief in him as a hero and ending with his utter corruption, and Eckhart pulls of this difficult performance with ease. Lastly we have Heath Ledger, the handsome, clean-cut star of *Brokeback Mountain* and *10 Things I Hate About You.* Ledger underwent a superhuman transformation in creating his performance as the Joker, isolating himself in a hotel room for a month to develop his every psychotic mannerism, from every lick of his lips to the blink of his eyes. It's unfortunate that this talented actor never lived to see the acclaims he achieved with this performance, going so far as to nab a posthumous Academy Award for it.

THE JOKER:

"Let's put a smile on that face!"

Batman interrogates The Joker. Warner Bros./DC Comics/The Kobal Collection

207

Captain America: The First Avenger

DIRECTED BY Joe Johnston
WRITTEN BY Christopher Markus (screenplay), Stephen McFeely (screenplay), Joe Simon (characters), Jack Kirby (characters)
STARRING Chris Evans, Tommy Lee Jones, Hugo Weaving, Hayley Atwell, Stanley Tucci
RELEASED July 19, 2011 (International)
RATED PG-13

Go team America! *Captain America: The First Avenger* is one film that can get your patriotism boiling! Set in 1942 during World War II, the men of America are called upon to save their country by enlisting in the military and fighting the good fight against the Nazi menace. Little do they know that a bigger and more powerful foe by the name of Red Skull (Hugo Weaving), Hitler's head of weaponry, is using a tesseract as an energy source to build uber-powerful weapons for his uber-powerful army to take over the world.

Steve Rogers (Chris Evans) is a skinny weakling who has repeatedly been denied admission into the army because of his numerous medical problems. After finally managing to talk his way in, he gets chosen for a special military project, a project that will create a new kind of super soldier. Buffed up and ready to go after the super-soldier serum does its trick, Rogers becomes Captain America and has to lead the United States in the battle against Red Skull and those darn Nazis!

Captain America: The First Avenger is based on Marvel's comic book character of the same name and can be considered somewhat of a prequel for the 2012 *Avengers* film. Captain America's humble, never-give-up-attitude and old school-style politeness make him one of the most loveable and relatable

STEVE ROGERS: **"I know this neighborhood. I got beat up in that alley. And that parking lot. And behind that diner."**

Steve Rogers is cheered by troops. Marvel/Paramount/The Kobal Collection

superheroes. He's an underdog; a nice guy who wants to do the right thing no matter the cost, and seeing him grow to become the hero he's always wanted to be leaves you with a warm, fuzzy feeling deep in your red, white, and blue heart.

The film is littered with great performances. Evans brings strength and relatability to Steve Rogers, Weaving is menacing as the Red Skull, and, as Col. Chester Philips, the always-dependable Tommy Lee Jones barks orders in a way that you, the viewer, want to jump on the front line so you don't disappoint him. Lastly, one of the best aspects of the film is that the female lead, Peggy Carter (Hayley Atwell), is truly an empowering character. As an English soldier who has already proven herself time and time again, she's treated like a respectable colleague rather than the afterthought that you often see the female leads devolved into. Even though she becomes the love interest to Captain America, she doesn't suddenly undergo a character castration and lose the strong core to her character, and she in no shape, form, or fashion becomes a hostage/liability, actually going as far as saving Captain America's butt a few times. Finally! A female love interest who isn't a hostage, and yes, I'm looking at you, Mary Jane! Maybe you should go save Spider-Man once in a while.

Between the strong but loveable Captain America, Peggy Carter, and the big action sequences scattered from start to finish, *Captain America: The First Avenger* satiates action junkie appetites as well as superhero fanatics.

Marvel/Paramount

Tron: Legacy

DIRECTED BY Joseph Kosinski
WRITTEN BY Edward Kitsis (screenplay/story), Adam Horowitz (screenplay/story), Brian Klugman (story), Lee Sternthal (story), Steven Lisberger (characters), Bonnie MacBird (characters)
STARRING Jeff Bridges, Garrett Hedlund, Olivia Wilde
RELEASED December 17, 2010
RATED PG-13

Tron: Legacy has unbeatable visual effects, which in turn create truly original action. The sights of the Grid are a spectacular blend of dark and light, like a rave held inside of a computer casing, and the sounds have a brilliance to match thanks in no small part to the amazing soundtrack

KEVIN FLYNN:

"The only way to win the game is not to play."

Sam (Garrett Hedlund) is the son of computer genius and star of the original *Tron*, Kevin Flynn (Jeff Bridges), who has spent the last twenty years MIA. In the first film, Flynn creates a virtual reality called the Grid and within it a computer program in his own likeness, named CLU (also Jeff Bridges), to keep the Grid running smoothly while Flynn is out in the real world.

So where has dear old daddy been all these years? The sequel picks up with Sam accidentally teleporting himself into the Grid and discovering that the elder Flynn has been trapped inside his own virtual reality all thanks to CLU, who turned just a little evil and conquered the computerized land. It turns out that CLU lured Sam onto the Grid in the hopes of using the portal he arrived in to travel into the real world with his digital army, using it to scrub out every "imperfection" he finds.

provided by Daft Punk. Another element that helps enhance the action is the non-human characters, all of whom are computer programs living on the Grid. Despite looking human, these programs don't shed any blood, only digital bits, which means that *Tron: Legacy* has some of the most brutally violent kills anyone will ever see in a Disney movie.

Walt Disney Productions

Sam, right, is challenged to a light cycle match.
Walt Disney Productions/The Kobal Collection

Lara Croft: Tomb Raider

DIRECTED BY Simon West
WRITTEN BY Sara B. Cooper (story), Mike Werb (story), Michael Colleary (story), Simon West (adaptation), Patrick Massett (screenplay), John Zinman (screenplay)
STARRING Angelina Jolie, Jon Voight, Iain Glen, Daniel Craig
RELEASED June 15, 2001
RATED PG-13

Lara Croft Tomb Raider: The Cradle of Life

DIRECTED BY Jan de Bont
WRITTEN BY Dean Georgaris (screenplay), Steven E. de Souza (story), James V. Hart (story)
STARRING Angelina Jolie, Gerard Butler, Chris Barrie
RELEASED July 25, 2003
RATED PG-13

When a person is in the business of treasure hunting, they should be ready to constantly have to defend those treasures from other greedy, not-so-nice treasure hunters. Case in point—Lara Croft (Angelina Jolie). Originating in the video game series *Tomb Raider,* Croft is constantly traveling the world to track down mystic artifacts before the aforementioned not-so-nice treasure hunters obtain them and use them to do not-so-nice things.

The first film finds her searching for an ancient triangle that will give her the power to control time; in the second, she's searching for an orb called the Cradle of Life that contains a map to Pandora's Box. Either way, she's in a race against time to find the macguffins before the baddies do.

The *Tomb Raider* films bring a variety of stunt work into play, including parachuting, scuba diving, and horseback riding. The first film also features an impressive sequence in which Croft starts off bungee jumping in her house for exercise, but as a group

BRYCE: "So, time to save the universe again then, is it?"

LARA CROFT: "Absolutely."

Lara Croft always keeps her cool. Paramount/The Kobal Collection

Paramount/Heritage Auctions

Angelina Jolie does most of her own stunts in her movies. Lawrence Gordon/Mutual Film/Paramount/Heritage Auctions/Alex Bailey

of armed infiltrators attacks, she uses the bungee cords to her advantage, jumping around like a monkey with machine guns. The sequel manages to take the insane stunt work to the next level, with perhaps the most memorable sequence being Lara Croft jumping from a Hong Kong skyscraper and floating to safety using a suit whose design seems inspired by flying squirrels.

Lara Croft is a motorcycle riding, leather wearing, gun slinging tomb raider; an independent gal who can take care of her own problems with two guns and a heaping helping of wiliness. Jolie brings a dry, cheeky sense of humor to the character, and her costars, including *Red Dwarf*'s Chris Barrie, do an admirable job supporting her. The *Tomb Raider* series is a worthy choice for the next action freak movie night, with its globe-trotting, treasure hunting escapades and light amounts of supernatural activities, all reminiscent of a modern Indiana Jones.

Hell on Heels

Angelina Jolie as the secret assassin Fox in *Wanted*.
Relativity/Spyglass/Universal/
The Kobal Collection

ANGELINA JOLIE

There's a woman considered one of the most desirable people alive and is sought after by every paparazzi and filmmaker around. No, I'm not talking about myself, I'm talking about Angelina Jolie! After a tumultuous young adulthood, Jolie has become a world-renowned actor known for her prowess as a thespian and her numerous bouts of charity work and good deeds. It's great that she does things for charities and all, but to an action movie freak, the most important thing is whether or not she can handle a gun, something that Jolie does not disappoint on.

Jolie has performed in films from all different genres, but what drew her into the action genre was *Lara Croft: Tomb Raider*. The physical challenges the part presented intrigued Jolie so she signed on and the rest is history. She went on to star as heroines in *Salt, Wanted,* and *Mr. & Mrs. Smith*, making her one of today's leading action actresses.

An action movie freak doesn't have to worry about terrible or cheesy performances in her action movies … at least not from *her* anyways. She is an actress first and foremost, having won several SAG Awards, Golden Globes, and even an Academy Award (Best Supporting Actress for *Girl, Interrupted*).

She's a woman who is in shape and more than a little wild, meaning that she does most of her own stunts, something you just don't see much out of Academy Award-winning actresses.

People often wish they could turn back time and redo something they messed up or take back something they said. Thanks to *Prince of Persia: The Sands of Time* unveiling the Dagger of Time, time control is now possible! Maybe you'd like to rewind history a few minutes so you don't make that stupid comment about your friend's botched boob job. Maybe your weekend was so fun you'd hate for it to end on Monday. Or maybe you *really* hated *Wild Wild West* and wish to God you could just unsee it. Well, wish no longer! The Dagger of Time can be yours for the easy price of 49,000 ruples!

Prince Dastan (Jake Gyllenhaal) discovers a rather unique looking

Prince of Persia: The Sands of Time

DIRECTED BY Mike Newell
WRITTEN BY Boaz Yakin (screenplay), Doug Miro (screenplay), Carlo Bernard (screenplay), Jordan Mechner (screen story/video game series "The Prince of Persia")
STARRING Jake Gyllenhaal, Gemma Arterton, Ben Kingsley
RELEASED May 28, 2010
RATED PG-13

Prince Dastan and Princess Tamina make an escape. Walt Disney Pictures/The Kobal Collection

PRINCE DASTAN:

"I know it hasn't been easy between us Garsiv, but still, we ARE brothers."

GARSIV:

"Touching words with my sword at your throat."

dagger, the Dagger of Time, as well as a gorgeous Princess Tamina (Gemma Arterton) during a raid on the holy city of Alamut. As you'd expect from the name, the Dagger of Time has the power to reverse time for up to one minute for anyone holding it. Also as expected, there are quite a few people who want to get their hands on this dagger (probably wanting to take back some boob job comments themselves) including Dastan's villainous uncle, Nizam, who wants to rewind time far back enough to make *him* king instead of his brother.

Despite a few little flaws here and there, like the plot being fairly threadbare and none of the leads actually being Persian, *Prince of Persia: The Sands of Time* is an enjoyable film. The fight choreography incorporates the kind of acrobatic swordplay that the modern video game series is known for, and "Chesty" Jake Gyllenhaal doesn't disappoint as an action hero, as he swings, flips, and slashes with the best of them. And this film is a Big Budget Hollywood Blockbuster with three capital Bs. The massive sets, the beautiful costumes, the special effects—everything's top-notch, and it's clear that top dollar went into creating the feel of an Ancient East riddled with magic and intrigue.

Kick-Ass

DIRECTED BY Matthew Vaughn
WRITTEN BY Jane Goldman (screenplay), Matthew Vaughn (screenplay), Mark Millar (comic book), John Romita Jr. (comic book)
STARRING Aaron Johnson, Nicolas Cage, Chloë Grace Moretz, Christopher Mintz-Plasse
RELEASED April 16, 2010
RATED R

Don't be fooled by Hit-Girl's young, innocent facade, because she'd just as soon gut you as look at you. She's like a cross between Strawberry Shortcake and John Rambo, making her a force to be reckoned with in the superhero film, *Kick-Ass*.

Kick-Ass is an adaptation of the comic book series created by Mark Millar and John Romita, Jr. The kicker is that the lead character isn't supposed to be Hit-Girl (Chloe Moretz) at all. She just ended up stealing the limelight and became a crowd favorite. The main protagonist is actually everyday geek, Dave (Aaron Johnson), who gets the wild idea to become a superhero. And his superhero name … is Kick-Ass! Not the best name, sure, but it does get extra points for its directness.

Ol' Kick-Ass has no special training at all and gets beaten up repeatedly. One day he runs into other superheroes, Big Daddy (Nicholas Cage) and Hit-Girl, who have, y'know, actual training. The trio works together to take down drug lord Frank D'Amico (Mark Strong). Though taking out this bad guy is just a step toward real superherodom for Kick-Ass, for Big Daddy and Hit-Girl, taking him out is about revenge, since D'Amico framed Big Daddy and destroyed his life.

The writers don't hold back when it comes to the amount of graphic violence and really inappropriate language, especially in regards to Hit-Girl. She says things that would make a sailor blush, and she brutishly slices and dices baddies better than a blood-drunk samurai, but she also receives her share of beatings. Nothing is spared just because she's a little girl, which has caused some controversy with some parent groups. But hey, a little controversy never hurt anyone, and if anything, it just gives action movie freaks all the more reason to watch *Kick-Ass*.

HIT GIRL:
"So, you wanna play?"

Hit-Girl about to give someone a taste of her fist. Marv Films/The Kobal Collection

Thor

DIRECTED BY Kenneth Branagh
WRITTEN BY Ashley Miller (screenplay), Zack Stenz (screenplay), Don Payne (screenplay), J. Michael Straczynski (story), Mark Protosevich (story), Stan Lee (comic book), Larry Lieber (comic book), Jack Kirby (comic book)
STARRING Chris Hemsworth, Natalie Portman, Tom Hiddleston, Anthony Hopkins
RELEASED May 6, 2011
RATED PG-13

THOR:

"This mortal form grows weak. I require sustenance!"

Marvel Studios has become more comfortable in branching out into the film industry with its superhero characters over the years. Marvel began by playing it safe with the one-two punch of *X-Men* and *Spider-Man,* then started working its way through its hero lineup until it brought on the lightning bolts by introducing *Thor.*

Thor (Chris Hemsworth) is the arrogant and battle-hungry son of Odin (Anthony Hopkins), king of Asgard and of the Norse Gods. After Thor blatantly disobeys his father's wishes, Odin decides that the boy needs to be taught a lesson and strips him of his powers, sending him to Earth to live amongst the humans. While Thor is "out of office," the Frost Giants decide to move in to destroy Asgard and Odin with the help of an insider, leaving Thor to figure out how to get his powers back and return to Asgard before it's too late.

Thor is an expensive movie, and it shows. Everything about it, from the sets to the costumes to the fight sequences and more, shine with the polish of a true Hollywood blockbuster. This polish extends to the action, with fight scenes depicting massive battles between super-powered beings unlike any other film to date. One fight scene in particular, a brawl featuring Thor and his friends facing off against a group of Frost Giants, really highlights a variety of stunt work and visual effects, with each of Thor's companions showing off their skills in different ways.

The cast helps keep the energy of the movie flowing as strong as Norse wine, with Hemsworth managing to balance Thor's early brattiness with enough charisma that the audience still roots for him even when he's throwing a super-powered tantrum, and Natalie Portman's skilled portrayal of Dr. Jane Foster keeps what could have otherwise been a stereotypically stiff scientist character both relatable and charming.

Superhero movies are big business, and few are as big as *Thor,* thanks in no small part to its great cast, incredible effects and action scenes, and deft balance between humor and character development.

Thor the mortal is unworthy of his hammer Mjolnir.
Marvel/Paramount/The Kobal Collection

Blade

DIRECTED BY Stephen Norrington
WRITTEN BY David S. Goyer
STARRING Wesley Snipes, Stephen Dorff, Kris Kristofferson
RELEASED August 21, 1998
RATED R

Blade clashes in more ways than one with vampire nemesis Deacon Frost, and all bets are off when his sunglasses are on.
New Line/The Kobal Collection

The initial installment introduces Deacon Frost (Stephen Dorff), a vampire who thinks humans should be corralled like cattle to serve and be fed to the vampires. Blade, however, thinks otherwise. Frost plans to perform a ritual that will turn him into an immortal vampire who can regenerate endlessly if hurt, and use this newfound power as the first step to overcoming the humans.

The whole series can be a little clichéd at times, but Blade disintegrates so many vampires in so many nifty ways that you'll often forgive the heapings of nacho cheesiness. For example, during one fight, Blade nonchalantly walks up to a vampire running to attack him, rips out his throat in one smooth motion, then turns to the next vampire and throws the chunk of throat in his face before proceeding to kick his ass. I don't know about you, but it's not every day that someone gets hit in the face with a ripped out vampire throat.

And when Blade puts on his sunglasses, all bets are off. Like Rambo's red bandana, those sunglasses are Blade's signature piece of clothing. He can brawl with the best of them when he's glasses-less, but once he has them on, it's like an invincibility star, meaning that anyone with two fangs and no pulse should probably vacate the area with extreme prejudice.

Blade Series

The human race has been saved! Everyone can breathe a little easier and go through their normal routines without having to worry about vampires trying to kill them and drink their blood. Blade (Wesley Snipes) has come to the rescue in his eponymous trilogy, protecting the world from all kinds of vicious vampires and malevolent mutants.

Blade was "born ready, mother fucker" in 1973 by Marvel Comics writer Marv Wolfman. While giving birth to him, Blade's mother was bitten by a vampire, thus creating a dhampir, a half breed human with vampire genes. He has all the strengths of a vampire and none of the weaknesses ... which sounds like a pretty peachy deal. In 1998, Blade made the jump to the big screen with the first film in the series.

BLADE:
"You give Frost a message from me. You tell him it's open season on all suckheads."

Blade II

DIRECTED BY Guillermo del Toro
WRITTEN BY David S. Goyer, Marv Wolfman
(character), Gene Colan (character)
STARRING Wesley Snipes, Kris Kristofferson,
Ron Perlman, Norman Reedus
RELEASED March 22, 2002
RATED R

New Line

Blade II ups the ante with a new race of super vampires called Reapers. These are stronger than a regular vampire (the better to catch their prey with), have three-way jaws that open up (the better to eat their prey with), are invulnerable to garlic and silver *and* have hearts encased in bone (the better to make their prey realize they don't stand a chance and bend over to kiss their asses goodbye). Regular vampires seek out Blade to form an uneasy partnership against the Reapers, with the vampires trying to save their own race, and Blade trying to save, yet again, the human race.

This film became the most successful financially out of the three *Blade* movies. The added terror of the super vamps is a whole new ball game, allowing for better fights and more creative sci-fi weaponry. And you've got the classic team of badasses slowly getting picked apart by a monster despite the fact that they've survived many missions together. What's the deal with these teams of badasses, anyway? They always *act* like they know what they're doing, but as soon as things get tough, they start dropping like flies, a la *Predator* or *Vampire Hunter D: Bloodlust.*

> **RAY CUMBERLAND:**
> "Say, how many people have you killed, Blade? Thirty? Forty? Fifty?"
> **BLADE:**
> "One thousand, one hundred and eighty two."

This time, in *Blade: Trinity*, Blade gets joined by a babe with a bow in the form of Abigail Whistler (Jessica Biel) and Hannibal King (a ripped Ryan Reynolds), two members of a vampire-hunting team known as the Nightstalkers. The addition of Biel's and Reynolds' new characters helps flesh out the *Blade* world a bit, breathing new life into the series with Reynolds' motormouth brand of humor and Biel's stoic portrayal of Abigail. It doesn't hurt that both of these new actors are extremely easy on the eyes, either, so no matter which gender you prefer, you're in for a treat.

The film follows Blade and the Nightstalker posse as they try to stop Drake, a.k.a Dracula (Dominic Purcell), from expanding the vampire race by creating more daywalkers. The Nightstalkers have created an airborne virus that is deadly to vampires and plan to wipe out the entire race for good. However, no one knows how the

Blade: Trinity

DIRECTED BY David S. Goyer
WRITTEN BY David S. Goyer, Marv Wolfman (character), Gene Colan (character)
STARRING Wesley Snipes, Jessica Biel, Ryan Reynolds, Kris Kristopherson, Parker Posey, Dominic Purcell
RELEASED December 8, 2004
RATED R

virus will affect Blade since he's a hybrid, leaving him to either figure out his own way to stop Drake or use the virus that could potentially kill him as well.

This movie does *not* mess around. The first several scenes are action sequence after action sequence, with the opening scene depicting Dracula pulling a vampire into the sand and decapitating him, then we get to watch Blade go on a magnificent vampire killing spree, *then* we see Abigail tricking some vamps into attacking her promptly before she busts out her sorta-lightsaber and burns their asses with 1.21 gigawatts of awesome. That's right, vamps! None of that damsel in distress stuff for this woman.

The whole *Blade* series is bloody, decapitating fun with an incredibly badass superhero. Because of *Blade's* success, Marvel grew enough confidence to make the *X-Men* and *Spider-Man* series, and for that the world is thankful.

Abigail (Biel) kicks some ass.
New Line Productions/The Kobal Collection/Diyah Pera

223

THE MILKSHAKE

One-Man Wrecking Crew!

It seems like this burger meal is pretty much complete, but it's still lacking one key ingredient. It's an item that can stand alone in many situations, is often anticipated with great joy, and is sometimes a meal within itself. That item ... is the milkshake! And in action movies, the one-man wrecking crew is that milkshake.

Milkshakes need nothing accompanying them to be delicious, but they do enhance the goodness of a meal, as a whole. Similarly, sometimes the heroes of an action movie are such loner badasses that they don't need anyone on their side, they can withstand anything on their own, and take down literally *endless* armies of enemies just to get where they need to go. These men (and women) are the action genre's one-man wrecking crews. Though most action heroes tend to fly pretty solo, these are the *extra-*solo heroes, the ones doing essentially everything all by their lonesome.

Every action movie is special, but there's something extra-special about seeing one lonely person take out an entire fleet of foes that'll get your blood boiling just a little bit more than normal. Maybe it's the fact that one person accomplishing such a seemingly impossible task really attracts people to root for them: it's the classic underdog story. These heroes shouldn't succeed, but somehow they inexplicably do thanks to the extra gallon of awesome pumping through their veins.

A lot of action films will have at least a pair, if not a whole team, of heroes trying to set things right again. The hero has someone to back them up, maybe bail

them out of a sticky firefight or rescue them if they're captured. It takes a lot of guts of steel and balls of adamantium to walk into a warehouse full of baddies who are foaming at the mouth to kill you, and this section is here to honor those adamantine-balled heroes. A one-man wrecking crew is just like it sounds: a lone person who wreaks havoc on a group of villains without help from anyone. Though they might get the occasional tidbit of assistance here or there, when it comes down to it, these guys and gals fly solo. So grab your milkshake and drink it up while reading about these one-man wrecking crews!

Steven Seagal proves he's a little more than "just a cook" in *Under Siege.* Warner Bros.

Die Hard

DIRECTED BY John McTiernan
WRITTEN BY Roderick Thorp (novel), Jeb Stuart (screenplay), Steven E. de Souza (screenplay)
STARRING Bruce Willis, Alan Rickman, Bonnie Bedelia
RELEASED July 15, 1988
RATED R

Die Hard Series

When action aficionados are asked what their favorite action movie is, most have two words to say: *Die Hard*! The whole series is stuffed with action like a Thanksgiving turkey thanks to the tough-as-nails, snarky-as-hell hero John McClane, played by Mr. Bruce Willis.

The success of the first film compelled the making of three sequels, with a fourth one in the works, totaling to five *Die Hard* films overall. As of this writing, the fifth film is to be titled *A Good Day to Die Hard* and features Willis reprising his role as McClane, which is good because it'd be blasphemy any other way. The film is due to release on Valentine's Day, 2013, which sounds like the best V-Day gift ever for action movie freaks!

On Christmas Eve, New York police officer John McClane arrives at Nakatomi Plaza in L.A. to attend a holiday party with his wife, Holly (Bonnie Bedelia). While McClane changes clothes for the shindig, Hans Gruber (Alan Rickman) swoops in, takes everyone hostage, and tries to open the Nakatomi vault.

McClane manages to evade capture and goes into survival mode, sneaking around the office building to assess the situation and assess his foot up a few terrorists' asses. Eventually, Gruber does a head count and notices a few of his men are

John McClane (Willis) is one of the most beloved action heroes. 20th Century Fox/Heritage Auctions

The stakes are raised when McClane finds out his wife is one of the terrorists' hostages. 20th Century Fox/Heritage Auctions

missing, leading to an intense game of cat and mouse.

Die Hard rocks for many reasons. It is literally one man saving the whole office building from a group of vicious murderers who wouldn't think twice about blowing their grandma away if she didn't bake them the right cookies. The only assistance McClane gets is via radio contact with a single police officer outside the tower, played by Reginald "Why Does This Guy Always Play a Cop?" VelJohnson. The cherry on top of the sundae is McClane's constant taunts toward the villains, including sending a message via a note pinned to the body of one of their dead comrades, which says: "Now I have a machine gun. Ho ho ho."

In this first installment, Bruce Willis is young, fit, and still has lots of hair. Bruce Willis with hair? Who knew? John McClane is probably Willis' best role, which is why he so often gets cast as McClane-esque characters. He has a good sense of timing for both action and sarcasm, and the strong doses of both are part of what makes *Die Hard* so

memorable.

Alan Rickman also gives a fantastic performance as Hans Gruber. So great, in fact, that he is often considered one of the most memorable villains in cinema history, with his flat, menacing voice, slick suit, and demeanor so cold he could chill wine.

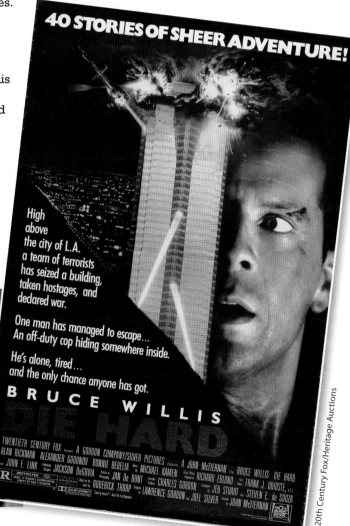

Villain Hans Gruber (Rickman, right) and his crew of terrorists.
20th Century Fox/Heritage Auctions

20th Century Fox/Heritage Auctions

227

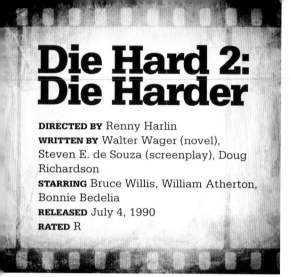

Die Hard 2: Die Harder

DIRECTED BY Renny Harlin
WRITTEN BY Walter Wager (novel),
Steven E. de Souza (screenplay), Doug
Richardson
STARRING Bruce Willis, William Atherton,
Bonnie Bedelia
RELEASED July 4, 1990
RATED R

This is more of the same fun and action as the first one. In fact, it is so similar to the first movie that even McClane makes a comment or two about it. Though it's not quite as sharp or action-packed as the original, it's still leagues above most movies, and definitely one to put on your family's list of Christmas movies.

JOHN McCLANE:

"Just once, I'd like a regular, normal Christmas. Eggnog, a fuckin' Christmas tree, a little turkey."

It's Christmas time again and John McClane is killing more terrorists in *Die Hard 2: Die Harder*, which has become something of a family tradition. "Hey kids, what do you want to do this Christmas?" McClane asks the kids, to which they reply, "We want to watch you single handedly kill some terrorists who've taken over a building." Well, pop the popcorn and bring out the sleeping bags, kiddos, because John McClane is back!

In the second installment *Die Hard 2: Die Harder*, McClane saves the day by running around an airport that's been captured by former U. S. army members who have seized the airport's air traffic controls in order to rescue a drug lord being flown in to stand trial in the U.S. No other planes can land or depart, which is bad news for McClane, since his wife is on one such plane. McClane tries to regain control of the monitors so that the flights can land before they run out of gas, all the while trying to keep the terrorists from rescuing the drug lord.

McClane makes a fiery escape via ejection seat in *Die Hard 2*.
20th Century Fox/The Kobal Collection

On a hot summer day in New York City, there's vengeance in the air. It seems Simon "Peter" Gruber, brother to Hans Gruber, has come to town looking for revenge in *Die Hard: With a Vengeance*.

For the first time, McClane unwillingly gets stuck with a partner in the form of civilian Zeus Carver (Samuel L. Jackson) as he tries to stop yet another terrorist. Simon leads the duo around town, solving riddles and getting into trouble, saying that he'll blow up an elementary school if both McClane and Carver don't do his bidding. While everyone's distracted by this wild goose chase, Simon enacts his real plan: stealing $140 billion in gold. Looks like family vengeance was just a cover story. Sorry Hans.

The third film steps away from the typical *Die Hard* formula of

Die Hard: With a Vengeance

DIRECTED BY John McTiernan
WRITTEN BY Jonathan Hensleigh, Roderick Thorp (certain original characters)
STARRING Bruce Willis, Jeremy Irons, Samuel L. Jackson
RELEASED May 19, 1995
RATED R

20th Century Fox/Heritage Auctions

one man + contained setting + group of terrorists = action. While it's a good film, it's kind of lackluster compared to the previous movies. On the plus side, however, Jackson and Willis make a fantastic combination; there's a great give-and-take to their dynamic that helps keep the film moving forward, even when it starts dragging a bit. Plus the addition of an extra lead helps up the tension. After all, at this point we know John McClane can't die—the filmmakers don't want to kill the golden goose. But his co-star sure as hell can.

ZEUS:

"What the hell's all this got to do with killing McClane?"

SIMON:

"Life has its little bonuses."

Live Free or Die Hard

DIRECTED BY Len Wiseman

WRITTEN BY Mark Bomback (screenplay/story), David Marconi (story), John Carlin (article), Roderick Thorp (certain original characters)

STARRING Bruce Willis, Justin Long, Timothy Olyphant

RELEASED June 27, 2008

RATED PG-13

MATT FARRELL:

"You just killed a helicopter with a car!"

JOHN McCLANE:

"I was out of bullets."

by hitting her with an SUV, sending her plummeting down an elevator shaft. Filming the fight was equally brutal, with Willis requiring stitches at one point thanks to an errant slash of Maggie Q's heels.

Overall, there are few series that continue for so long without seeing bizarre degradation in quality or strange new plot twists to help keep the franchise "fresh," but the *Die Hard* series is one of the few that keeps it fresh and fantastic without veering off in bizarre directions. Although fans may disagree as to just how good the various sequels are, there's one thing we can all agree on: *Die Hard* kicks ass.

Returning 13 years after the last film, with more punch, more enthusiasm, and more Maggie Q, is the fourth film, *Live Free or Die Hard*. Critics hailed the film as surpassing the third, and Willis has even gone so far as to say he thought it was better than the first. Opinions aside, it's certainly wilder than the first. After all, in *Live Free or Die Hard*, we see McClane pulling off near-superhuman stunts like blowing up a helicopter by ramping a car into it. A car, people!

The villains' targets have gotten bigger and bigger throughout the series. They go after a lone building in *Die Hard*, then an airport, then NYC, and finally they aim to take down the entire East Coast in the fourth film. It's up to McClane and expert hacker Matt Farrell (Justin Long) to locate the cyber terrorists before everyone's internet gets erased.

Live Free or Die Hard is filled with some gritty brawls, including a lengthy battle between McClane and Mai Linh (Maggie Q). After the two have whaled on each other for a while, McClane finishes the job

Out of bullets? Do things the John McClane way and kill a 'copter with a car.
20th Century Fox/The Kobal Collection/Frank Masi

BRUCE WILLIS

One action star who most certainly became famous for his acting talent rather than his martial arts skills or big brawny physique is Bruce Willis. The action genre needs a variety of action heroes, and Willis has a knack for adding warmth and character to otherwise cold-hearted killing machines. While most action heroes will first endear themselves to the audience based on their skill as a hero, Willis flips this approach on its head by assembling a character the audience will like for his personality first, and *then* like because he can kill a dozen men who have hijacked a high rise building.

Willis made a name for himself as an action star with John McClane in *Die Hard*. He had the freedom to ad lib a lot of his dialogue throughout the film series, and it's these antagonistic wisecracks that helped shape John McClane into the legendary character he is today.

Willis' resume includes big hits like *The Fifth Element*, *Die Hard*, *Pulp Fiction*, and *The Sixth Sense*, and that's just a drop of the hat compared to the more than seventy films he's starred in. Bruce Willis is a man who knows how to entertain, and whether he's a cop dealing with terrorists or a cab driver in the distant future, he brings his trademark brand of sarcastic wit to the table to help bring these characters to life.

Bruce Willis as the sardonic and iconic action hero John McClane.
20th Century Fox/The Kobal Collection/Peter Sorel

Commando

DIRECTED BY Mark L. Lester
WRITTEN BY Jeph Loeb (story), Matthew Weisman (story), Steven E. de Souza (story and screenplay)
STARRING Arnold Schwarzenegger, Rae Dawn Chong, Dan Hedaya
RELEASED Oct. 4, 1985
RATED R

John Matrix mows down anyone in the way of him getting back his kidnapped daughter. 20th Century Fox/Heritage Auctions/Bruce McBroom

JOHN. It seems like you just can't be a true action hero unless your name is John, the MANLIEST of men's names. Just think about all the action hero characters whose name is John: John Spartan (*Demolition Man*), Detective John Kimble (*Kindergarten Cop*), John McClane (*Die Hard*), Johnny Utah (*Point Break*), John Rambo (*Rambo*), John Connor (*Terminator*), and John Matrix (*Commando*). My deepest sympathy to any action-hero-hopefuls out there who aren't named John because it looks like your chances of becoming an action hero are slim. Now, if you were to change your name, it might significantly increase your odds of being able to break a friend out of a jungle prison or liberate a group of hostages from a European terrorist.

In *Commando*, we have John Matrix (Arnold Schwarzenegger) single handedly taking down a metric butt-ton of people in an exemplary show of what it is to be a one-man wrecking crew. Now, you may ask, exactly how much is a metric butt-ton? There'll be a point in the movie where you'll say to yourself, "Jeez! How many people did he just kill!?!" A metric

butt-ton, that's how many.

John Matrix has it pretty good. He has his health, a nice house in the fresh mountain air, and a cool daughter (Alyssa Milano) who hasn't been kidnapped. Oops, scratch that last one, because right as Matrix is finishing up another round of cutting down some trees for no reason, his old military buddies show up and swipe her. Turns out they've gone bad, real bad, and they're working with some other real bad dudes to try to coerce Matrix into assassinating someone for them. As kind as that offer is, Matrix turns it down and spends the rest of the movie killing everyone until he finds his daughter by sheer process of elimination.

Arnold's John Matrix character is a lot like John Rambo. Both have retired from their military careers of annihilating people, both are trying just to live normal lives, and both have their own hype men to talk about how badass they are. Where Rambo had Col. Trautman to tell people they'd need more body bags, Matrix has Col. Kirby to tell people to "Expect WWIII."

Commando is the kind of action movie that really gets your blood pumping, but it's important to note that it definitely gets liberal with

ARIUS:

ARIUS: "Your father appears to be cooperating. You will be back with him soon. Won't that be nice?"

JENNY: "Not nearly as nice as watching him smash your face in."

Matrix gets the upper hand on former teammate Bennett (Vernon Wells).
20th Century Fox/Heritage Auctions/Bruce McBroom

Being a man of few words, Matrix often lets his explosions do the talking.
20th Century Fox/Heritage Auctions/Bruce McBroom

the boundaries of realism. For example, Matrix has some superhuman-strength moments, like pulling a metal chain and padlock off of a gate with his bare hands or ripping a seat out of a car without a struggle. My personal favorite is when he body slams a telephone booth with someone still in it trying to make a call!

For every silly unrealistic act, there is an act of equal or greater awesomeness. Matrix is talking to one of the kidnappers. The poor stupid guy says, "If you want your kid back, you've got to cooperate with us, right?" Then, without any hesitation, Matrix turns and says, "Wrong!" Then he shoots the guy right in the head. Can't bully him into cooperating! If anything, the kidnappers should cooperate with him if they value their lives.

Hard Target

DIRECTED BY John Woo
WRITTEN BY Chuck Pfarrer
STARRING Jean-Claude Van Damme, Lance Henriksen, Yancy Butler
RELEASED August 20, 1993
RATED R

NATASHA BINDER: "What kind of a name is Chance?" CHANCE BOUDREAUX: "Well ... my momma took one ..."

Speaking of one-man wrecking crews, Jean-Claude Van Damme wrecks some major stuff in *Hard Target*. Well, JCVD doesn't completely take out everyone by himself, he does get a little bit of help from the absurd mullet he's sporting. Seriously, that thing is so over-moussed it could stop a sniper's bullet.

In *Hard Target*, Chance Boudreaux (JCVD) and his mullet happen to save a woman, Natasha (Yancy Butler), from being mugged by using his superb martial arts skills. Impressed by his skills and in spite of his hair, she offers him a job as her bodyguard while she searches for her missing father. They soon find themselves in some deep doo-doo when they find out her dad was a target of villain Fouchon's (Lance "Pretty good for a human" Henriksen) hunting game.

Fouchon and his minions run an operation where bored rich people looking for a little excitement can pay a bunch of money to hunt a real person with whatever weapon they want, *Most Dangerous Game* style. To fill out the

Chance Boudreaux: 1; rattlesnake: 0. Universal/The Kobal Collection

selection of prey for his sadistic game, Fouchon selects homeless men, preferably with war experience and no family, as the targets. As Chance gets closer to uncovering their little game, he becomes a target himself, although the mercenaries quickly realize that he's no easy target like the rest of their prey. In fact, you could say Chance is a ... hard target.

The distinguished John Woo, known for his intricate stylized action sequences, chose *Hard Target* as his American directorial debut. Conversely, *Hard Target* is the first American film directed by a Chinese director, and things work out well for everyone, seeing as how *Hard Target* is a nonstop thrill ride. The combination of JCVD/John Woo is a tasty one; the style of these two action icons blend well together. Once Woo worked with JCVD for a little bit, he increased the number of action sequences in the film, knowing that JCVD could handle it.

Henrikson's Fouchon is an especially cold-hearted son of a bitch, bringing a legitimate sense of menace to the film. For example, one of his minions gets bit by a snake in a trap Chance sets up, and he's dying in agony. Fouchon's thoughts? "If you would die quieter, and pick up the pace, Boudreaux would have less time for these kinds of surprises." Harsh, dude!

So sure, the story is barebones and JCVD can't act worth a damn, but you're not a true action freak if you let that deter you from an action film. *Hard Target* possesses an explosive finale, as well as other insane action spectacles, JCVD, and his mullet—all worth enduring a little cheesy acting for.

Under Siege

DIRECTED BY Andrew Davis
WRITTEN BY J.F. Lawton
STARRING Steven Seagal, Gary Busey, Tommy Lee Jones
RELEASED October 9, 1992
RATED R

Lessons can be found in anything; all you have to do is pay attention and you can learn something. Take *Under Siege,* for example, which teaches us that, if someone is asking for the highest-ranking officer onboard a ship, don't fess up to being that person because more likely than not, you're bending over and painting a target on your ass, complete with a big neon sign that says, SHOOT ME SO THE PLOT CAN CONTINUE.

In *Under Siege, a* group of mercenaries led by ex-CIA agent Bill Strannix (Tommy Lee Jones) and Commander Krill (Gary Busey) take over the American battleship USS Missouri so they can steal the ship's nuclear weapons and sell them on the black market. But what they don't foresee is the power of a simple cook, Casey Ryback (Steven Seagal), to thwart their plan, because, as it turns out, Ryback is no ordinary cook. The man's a chief petty officer and former Navy Seal with special weapons training, meaning he has just as much skill with a blade as a spatula. And he's a *damn* good cook. So to stop Strannix and Krill, Ryback has to slink around the ship and take out an endless sea of nameless henchmen ... like *Die Hard,* but on a boat!

Under Siege is one of Seagal's best works. His brand of humor, conventional wisdom, and hapkido skills are sometimes at odds with the other happenings in the films he's in, but in *Under Siege* they're the perfect spice to the gumbo of the movie. It helps that his co-stars are Tommy Lee Jones and Gary Busey, since no one can play a man teetering on the edge of sanity like Busey, and Jones is one of those magic "never fails" actors that, no matter how ridiculous the script or unbelievable the premise, he always gives a great performance. In *Under Siege,* it's especially fun to watch his character grow progressively more unhinged as things begin to unravel.

If action movie freaks want to add a Seagal film to their collection, *Under Siege* is one of the best, as strong performances give it strength of action and humor that's missing in lesser films.

JORDAN TATE:
"So who are you? Are you, like, some special forces guy or something?"
CASEY RYBACK:
"Nah. I'm just a cook."

The movie culminates with a knife fight between Ryback and Strannix.
Warner Bros./Regency/The Kobal Collection

STEVEN SEAGAL

Need a ride to the bank? Steven Seagal will take you to the bank ... the blood bank. DUM DUM DUM!

Seagal, known for his black ponytail, squinty eyes, and six-foot-four-inch frame, has starred in a variety of films such as *Above the Law, Under Siege,* and *Hard to Kill,* most of which see him as the hero, although he does mix it up occasionally with a villainous role or two, as in *Machete.* Unlike many other action heroes, Seagal frequently portrays a soft-spoken, kind, almost timid man in most of his films, and often will incorporate Buddhist philosophies into his characters, as Seagal himself is a major believer in Buddhism. But underneath this peaceful surface broils a storm of ass kicking that no villain is prepared for.

He brings a similarly unique style of fighting to his roles, specializing in Aikido, a counter-attack focused style of Japanese martial arts using the opponent's own body weight against them to incapacitate them. Seagal is a 7th Dan in Aikido, allowing him to turn his talent into a lifelong career entertaining millions of people on the big screen.

Steven Seagal from *Marked for Death*, considered one of his best films.
20th Century Fox/The Kobal Collection

GoldenEye

DIRECTED BY Martin Campbell
WRITTEN BY Ian Fleming (characters), Michael France (story), Jeffrey Caine (screenplay), Bruce Feirstein (screenplay)
STARRING Pierce Brosnan, Sean Bean, Izabella Scorup
RELEASED November 17, 1995
RATED PG-13

James Bond is the epitome of a one-man wrecking crew. There have been approximately twenty-three films featuring Sir Ian Fleming's secret agent James Bond—twenty-three! In virtually every film, Bond spoils a baddie's plan by himself. These films make up the longest-running series in history, starting with the first release in 1962 and continuing to present day with *Skyfall* being released in 2012.

Six different actors have played Bond over the years, with constant disagreement as to who is the best. Chronologically, Pierce Brosnan is the fifth James Bond and makes his film debut in *GoldenEye.* Brosnan plays a very likable, gentlemanly pervert of a hero. He's smooth, obsessed with double entendres, and can take down the baddies like no one else.

GoldenEye finds Bond combating a Russian crime syndicate group that has taken control of one of the GoldenEye satellites to steal money from the Bank of England. The group's plan would also erase all of the bank's financial records,

destroying evidence of the crime, along with Britain's economy.

The stunt work in this film is truly spectacular from start to finish. It opens with stuntman Wayne Michaels bungee jumping 720 feet off of a dam and setting a record for highest jump off of a fixed structure. How Michaels gathered up the nerve to do this jump is beyond mortal comprehension—just the camera shot overlooking the edge of the dam is enough to induce nausea in most. The man deserves a cookie. There are plenty more high-octane action scenes in the rest of the film, including explosions, hand-to-hand

Bond steals a tank to chase a renegade Russian general.
Danjaq/Eon/UA/The Kobal Collection/Keith Hamshere

fights, and an insane vehicular chase involving a tank hunting down a car through the streets of Moscow. There are a lot of good Bond films, but *GoldenEye* is definitely one to keep an *eye* on.

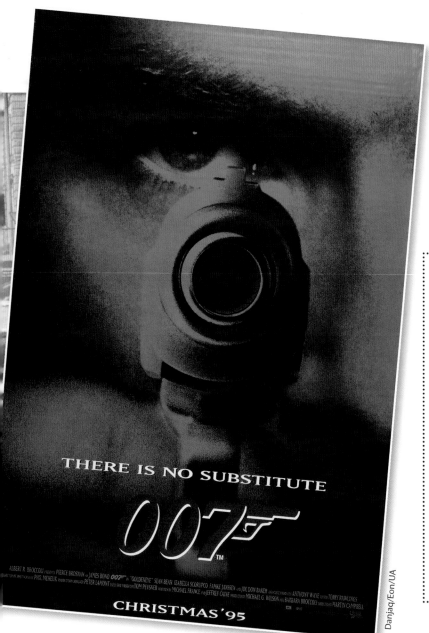

THERE IS NO SUBSTITUTE

007

ALBERT R. BROCCOLI presents PIERCE BROSNAN as JAMES BOND 007 in "GOLDENEYE" SEAN BEAN IZABELLA SCORUPCO FAMKE JANSSEN and JOE DON BAKER director of photography PHIL MÉHEUX production designer PETER LAMONT edited by TOM PEVSNER written by MICHAEL FRANCE and JEFFREY CAINE associate producer ANTHONY WAYE editor TERRY RAWLINGS produced by MICHAEL G. WILSON and BARBARA BROCCOLI directed by MARTIN CAMPBELL

CHRISTMAS '95

Danjaq/Eon/UA

XENIA ONATOPP:

"You don't need the gun, commander."

JAMES BOND:

"Well, that depends on your definition of safe sex."

Best Escape

The crazy s.o.b. Bond is trapped up on a high isolated cliff with a group of baddies firing at him. He rides a motorcycle off the cliff chasing after an airplane that took off (without a pilot). The airplane heads downward to crash at the bottom, but Bond doesn't care. He rides off the cliff and streamlines his body in order to catch the plane. Miraculously, he manages to get in the pilot seat and pull the plane up before it crashes, escaping the baddies. Escaping isn't enough for Bond, though. The building he left behind full of baddies blows up as he flies off into the sunset. That's a slap in the face for villains everywhere!

Raiders of the Lost Ark

DIRECTED BY Steven Spielberg
WRITTEN BY Lawrence Kasdan
(screenplay), George Lucas (story), Philip
Kaufman (story)
STARRING Harrison Ford, Karen Allen,
Paul Freeman, John Rhys-Davies
RELEASED June 12, 1981
RATED PG

A majority of action films are not meant for children's eyes, and if they were, it'd make this action freak wonder about the quality of the action. However, *Raiders of the Lost Ark* finds a way to entertain the adults with legitimate grown-up action, but keeps it fun and clean so that the little ones can watch it, too, shaping the perfect film for family movie night.

Indiana Jones (Harrison Ford), also known as Indy, is a proper, suit-wearing professor of archeology by day and a whip wielding, hat wearing, fist-fighting adventurer by night. There are four films in the *Indiana Jones* series, and even a series as legendary as this still falls victim to the notion of the diminishing returns of sequels, with the first of the series continuing to be the favorite among viewers. However, all of the films enjoyed great success both financially and critically, causing the franchise to branch out in the forms of novels, comics, video games, and a television series.

The birth of the franchise starts with

Raiders of the Lost Ark, where Indy finds himself in a race against the Nazis to find the Ark of the Covenant, a biblical item that holds fragments of the Ten Commandments. The Nazis want possession of it so that their army will become invincible, and invincible Nazis is something Indy just won't stand for.

Indy (Ford) tries to outsmart the booby-trapped golden idol he's after... Lucasfilm LTD/Paramount/Heritage Auctions

But he's not quite successful. Lucasfilm LTD/Paramount/Heritage Auctions

Being an adventure film, a lot of the action comes from Indy getting himself into some tight places where he's forced to think his way out. He escapes from a sealed-off room filled with hordes of snakes, outruns a gigantic boulder, and deals with more than a few tarantulas. How nice of the filmmakers to include every creepy-crawly critter they could think of.

Indy's worries don't stop with animals, however, as he frequently has to face off against Nazis or other unsavory people, usually winning out by virtue of his wits rather than his fist-fighting skills.

INDIANA:

"I hate snakes, Jock! I hate 'em."

For example, one of Indy's most well-known fight scenes is a brief moment where a swordsman flamboyantly shows off his skills with a scimitar, which Indy responds to by pulling out a pistol and shooting the guy before wandering off. Ford was suffering from dysentery and was too tired to fight the baddie, so he came up with a new direction for the fight scene: "Let's just shoot the fucker." Director Spielberg agreed, and that little change became a defining moment for Indy and the film.

The American Film Institute classified *Raiders of the Lost Ark* as No. 66 in the "Greatest Movies of All Time" list in 2007. It received numerous awards and has been parodied and referenced in other material probably thousands of times. Plain and simple, it's a top-ranking action-adventure film and definitely one of the very few PG action movies to watch.

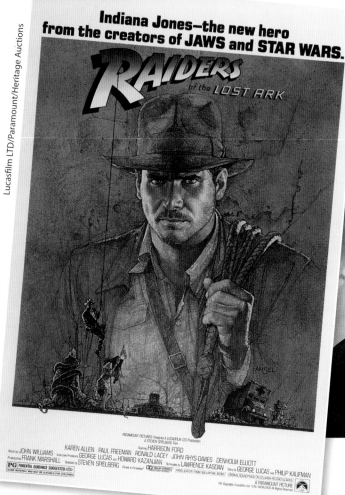

Lucasfilm LTD/Paramount/Heritage Auctions

Indy and former love Marion Ravenwood (Allen).
Lucasfilm LTD/Paramount/Heritage Auctions

Kill Bill Vol. 1 and 2

DIRECTED/WRITTEN BY Quentin Tarantino
STARRING Uma Thurman, Lucy Liu,
Vivica Fox, Daryl Hannah, David
Carradine
PART 1: RELEASED October 10, 2003
PART 2: RELEASED April 16, 2004
RATED R

There's hardly anything that will piss
off a woman more than trying to kill her
on her wedding day. There's a reason a
television show called *Bridezillas* exists.
But if an assassin *has* to kill the bride on
her day of glory, he'd better make damn
sure the job is finished, or he'll have one
very cross lady knocking at his door.

Kill Bill originally was one film, but since
it was over four hours long, it was split into
two volumes. *Kill Bill Vol. 1* is a ball-busting
flick that immediately grabs a viewer's
attention by showing a bride (Uma
Thurman) in her lovely wedding dress,
hair done, veil on, looking so pretty on her
very special day … except that she's been
beaten to a bloody pulp at the hands of
her group of ex-muchachos, the Deadly
Viper Assassination Squad. Oh, and then
she gets shot in the head. And *then,* to
add insult to injury, the audience finds out
she's pregnant. When a film opens with
a pregnant bride being shot in the head,
you know it's playing for keeps.

**The Bride's ball-busting skills
help her fight off a Yakuza
army.** A Band Apart/Miramax/The
Kobal Collection

THE BRIDE:

"You and I have unfinished business."

BILL:

"Baby, you ain't kidding."

Thurman plays "The Bride," who is one of the most merciless, heartless beyotches you'll ever lay eyes on. Then again, the people she's after *did* try to kill her on her wedding day, killed her child (or so she thinks), and killed her whole wedding party, groom included. *Volume 1* of the *Kill Bill* saga sees the beginning of The Bride's journey of revenge as she methodically takes apart every member of the Deadly Viper Assassination Squad.

In *Volume 2,* The Bride catches up to the rest of the group including their leader, Bill (David Carradine). The two are ex-lovers and Bill is the father of The Bride's child, a child who, The Bride discovers, is alive and well, being raised by Bill himself.

An homage to the exploitation films of yesteryear, *Kill Bill Vol. 1 and 2* were both written and directed by Quentin Tarantino, so the films are filled with sequences of truly unique filmmaking, such as the animated sequence explaining O-Ren's (Lucy Liu) origin, as well as hopscotching between over-the-top violence and *Gilmore Girls* levels of overly verbose conversations. The frequent monologues may turn off some viewers, but rest assured, there's plenty of action to be had, as The Bride's reign of vengeance is filled with enough gore to slake the thirst of even the most bloodthirsty of action fans.

She's the true epitome of the one-man wrecking crew, at one point taking out the Crazy 88, a gang of 88 sword-wielding lunatics, all in one go. Hell, even burying her alive doesn't stop her. This is a chick with blood on her hands and revenge in her heart.

Rumble in the Bronx

DIRECTED BY Stanley Tong
WRITTEN BY Edward Tang, Fibe Ma
STARRING Jackie Chan, Anita Mui, Françoise Yip, Marc Akerstream
RELEASED Feb. 23, 1996
RATED R

The phrase "one-man wrecking crew" can undeniably be used to describe Jackie Chan in *Rumble in the Bronx.* He destroys so much stuff he's like a Chinese hulk. With no help from anyone, he efficiently incapacitates half of New York, and takes out not one, but *two* gangs of criminals, all while he is supposed to be on vacation!

Keung (Chan) takes down a punk. Golden Harvest/New Line/The Kobal Collection

There are multiple forces at play in *Rumble in the Bronx*. Jackie Chan plays a Hong Kong cop, Keung, who's visiting New York to attend his uncle's wedding. Trouble starts immediately when a gang decides to hold a street race on top of the other cars parked in the street. Keung messes up their race in order to save his uncle's car, leaving the uncle thrilled, but the gang pissed. He runs into the same gang several more times and thwarts their plans for criminal activity. Finally, after several ass beatings from Keung, the gang decides to form a truce so that they won't wake up with swollen eyes and lips anymore. That's when a second gang comes in.

This much larger, much more vicious group of criminals are in the middle of an illegal diamond exchange when it goes terribly wrong and someone from gang No. 1 ends up with the diamonds. Now that gang No. 1 is friends with Keung, they call on him to help protect them against gang No. 2.

Let it be known that Jackie Chan is an amazing stuntman! He did all of his own stunts for this film and ended up with a broken ankle fairly early in filming, but that didn't stop him. He continued on with his leg in a cast, covered in a sock colored like his shoe. In fact, several stunt doubles sustained broken limbs and injuries during filming. That's a testimony as to how crazed the action is.

Though *Rumble in the Bronx* isn't especially violent or gory, it is high-class entertainment, with a heavy mix of martial arts and Chan's prop-combat. After watching this movie, viewers will never see a jacket as just a *jacket* anymore; they'll see it as a potential means of destruction.

AH KEUNG:

"I hope next time we meet, we will be drinking tea."

Golden Harvest/New Line

5

Hell on Heels

CYNTHIA ROTHROCK

Cynthia Rothrock may not be as well known as Jackie Chan and some of the other actors in this book, but she's certainly left her mark in the world of action. Starting martial arts training when she was 13, she used her talents to make a name for herself in films.

She was discovered by a film production company that was looking for the "next Bruce Lee." What an honor that they found what they were looking for in Rothrock! She was then cast in *Yes, Madam* with Michelle Yeoh and, with that film being a success, she decided to stay in Hong Kong to make several more titles before returning to the United States to continue her film career. She is the rare case of someone becoming famous overseas before becoming known in her home country.

Throughout Rothrock's martial arts career, she achieved six black belts in various forms of disciplines, won World Karate Champion in Forms & Weapons five times, and was the undefeated middleweight kickboxing/weapons lady champion five years in a row. She has since retired from making films or competing in tournaments and is teaching martial arts, passing on her awesomeness. She was in more than 40 titles during her movie career, enhancing the reputation of the action genre, as well as women as a whole.

Rothrock, in a scene from *Lady Dragon*, continues to pass on her awesomeness through teaching martial arts. Rapi Films/The Kobal Collection

The Axercise fitness system, as seen in *Cobra*, is now available for a limited time! Get those sleek, toned arms and flat abs in no time by joining the Axercisers cult! All you need is an axe in each hand. Good! Now clank them to the rhythm, just like they do over and over in *Cobra*. Hurry! The offer ends soon!

Okay, so they might not really be called Axercisers, but this group of axe-wielding baddies do stand around banging their axes together an awful lot so they should be.

The Axercisers are but a single piece of the delicious pie that is *Cobra*. The other pieces are a serial killer called the Night Slasher (Brian Thompson), leader of the Axerciser cult and headcase extraordinaire. He's obsessed with killing off society's weaklings,

Cobra

DIRECTED BY George P. Cosmatos
WRITTEN BY Paula Gosling (novel),
Sylvester Stallone (screenplay)
STARRING Sylvester Stallone, Brigitte
Nielsen, Reni Santoni
RELEASED May 23, 1986
RATED R

As a renegade cop, Cobretti does things his way to clean up crime. Warner Bros./The Kobal Collection

wanting to ensure the survival of only the fittest. Well, if he was looking for the fittest ... he found it. Lieutenant Marion Cobretti a.k.a Cobra (Sylvester Stallone) is on a mission to stop the Night Slasher and his Axercisers by protecting the one witness, Ingrid (Brigitte Nielsen), who can identify the baddies.

Cobra suffers from being completely under rated. With a striking tag line like, "Crime is a disease. Meet the cure," it tells the audience exactly what to expect: a film bursting at the seams with crime-cleansing action! Of course, it's not an Oscar-winning masterpiece; the villains are one-dimensional and the action is anything but realistic. But that's what makes it so good! After all, the goal of any good action movie isn't to win Oscars for being that year's Most Touching Film. Action movies are supposed to show off crazy stunts and good prevailing in the face of overwhelming evil, and that's exactly what Cobra does.

Cobra himself is the epitome of the tough hero. He spits out snazzy catch phrases like a child spitting out broccoli, carries the perfect "I don't give a shit what the rules say, I'm going to blow you away" attitude, and tolerates precisely zero crap from the bad guys, whether they have one hostage or one hundred.

This film is a shoe-in for one-man wrecking machine. According to IMDB.com, the body count for the film equals 52, and almost 100 percent of that is Cobra. He demolishes an entire gang of Axercisers and the Night Slasher by himself, and I think it's time to give credit where credit is due. Let *Cobra* slither onto your screen and you won't be disappointed.

CHIEF HALLIWELL:
"Cobretti, do you know you have an attitude problem?"

MARION COBRETTI:
"Yeah, but it's just a LITTLE one!"

Warner Bros./Heritage Auctions

6

Man of Action

SYLVESTER STALLONE

The legendary Sylvester Stallone is one of the greatest action stars of all time. Carolco/The Kobal Collection

From the very beginning of Sylvester Stallone's acting career, he's been getting in on the action, although some of it was a *very* different kind of action seeing as how his very first role was a soft-core porno. After that, however, he found his true niche as an action hero.

Stallone has brought to life some of the most iconic characters in movie history, including his two most well-known roles, John Rambo and Rocky Balboa. These two film series reeled in huge financial success and earned many awards and recognitions, with *Rocky* propelling Stallone into worldwide fame, and *First Blood (Rambo I)* establishing him as a bonafide badass. After that, he's had an almost endless line of action movie roles, with such films as *Tango & Cash, Cobra, Demolition Man, Cliffhanger, Judge Dredd,* four more *Rocky* films, three more *Rambo*s, two *Expendables,* and a partridge in a pear tree.

Stallone isn't just a pile of muscles with a pretty face; the man has brains to go along with his brawn. He's not only written, but also directed, many of the film's he's starred in. Hearing the man discuss the thought process behind each of them really shows the amount of insight and passion he has for his projects.

Out of all the actors out there who excel in action roles, Stallone is easily one of, if not *the,* most influential actor in the genre. Time and time again he delivers solid work in the action genre whether it's through writing, directing, or acting, and while Schwarzenegger moved on to politics and let his physique go soft, Stallone was out making *Rambo* (*IV*) and *The Expendables*. After all, being an action hero is where Stallone belongs. A true testament to that is the fact that today, at the age of sixty-six, he's performing in major action roles, doing stunts that men half his age would shy away from.

So on behalf of all the other action movie freaks out there, I say thank you, Sly! Here's to sixty-six more years of action movie making!

Taken

DIRECTED BY Pierre Morel
WRITTEN BY Luc Besson, Robert Mark Kamen
STARRING Liam Neeson, Maggie Grace, Famke Janssen
RELEASED January 30, 2009
RATED PG-13

Never has the expression "Don't talk to strangers" ever been as true as it is in *Taken*. After some punks kidnap Liam Neeson's daughter, the Liam drops the hammer and rules this movie as he runs around Paris kicking every single bad guy's ass all by his lonesome! It's not like he is being unfair, either—he gives them ample warning as to what is going to happen. The kidnappers just don't believe him until it is too late.

Neeson plays Bryan Mills, a concerned and crafty father whose daughter gets kidnapped by Albanian slave traffickers while vacationing in Paris. BOY DID THEY PICK THE WRONG GUY TO MESS WITH! Mills is a former CIA agent and does not have money, but what he does have is a very particular set of skills ... skills that make him a nightmare for guys like them. What kind of skills? We're talking about being able to hand 10 guys their asses at one time, while they're armed with guns and he's armed with a shoe! We're talking about tracking a dude down based on his reflection in a picture he was taking. We're talking about enough skills to basically level Paris while searching for his daughter, that's what.

What I've described above is basically the entire movie: Girl goes to Paris, girl gets kidnapped, Bryan Mills goes on a rampage to save her. The end. So simple, yet sooooo GLORIOUS! So while *Taken* is not exactly complicated in the story department, it really doesn't matter. The action from the one-man wrecking crew keeps the bodies stacking and the audience's blood pumping. After all, saving a girl from human traffickers is a worthwhile mission that the audience can really rally behind, and seeing Liam Neeson smash faces and electrocute bad guys ... well, it just doesn't get old. The man promises to kill anyone who crosses him, and he stands by his word. Hard not to respect that.

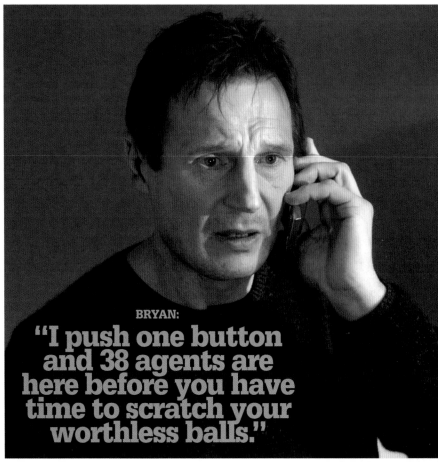

BRYAN:
"I push one button and 38 agents are here before you have time to scratch your worthless balls."

To get his daughter back, Mills does anything he needs to using his special set of skills. Europa Corp/The Kobal Collection

INDEX

Photo by Jennifer Kelley Lublin.

ABOUT THE AUTHOR

Katrina Hill is, first and foremost, a lover of all things action. She's been in love with the action genre since a young age, taking influence from action stars both new and old, from Stallone and Schwarzenegger to Statham, and even independent action stars such as Tony Jaa. Katrina created and runs the website www.actionflickchick.com, and has quickly became known as the go-to source for action movie news, reviews, and interviews. She has accumulated a following of over 150,000 on Twitter (@actionchick), has given several panel presentations in front of thousands at San Diego Comic-Con International, and also writes freelance for other publications such as MTV Geek and GeekNation.

ALL AROUND MOVIE FREAK?

CHECK OUT OUR OTHER "MOVIE FREAK" TITLES.

"I'll be back." – The Terminator, The Terminator (1984)

To the movies, that is. And so will you with the help of *Sci-Fi Movie Freak*, a celebration of some of the greatest science-fiction movies of all time. Your inner geek will freak finding everything from classics like *Metropolis*, *Forbidden Planet*, and *2001: A Space Odyssey* to modern movies including *Avatar*, *Moon*, and *Inception*, and even the entertaining "failures" like *Robot Monster*, *Gammera the Invincible*, and *Battlefield Earth*.

Item# W5966 · $21.99

You'll scream with delight as you take in this gloriously gruesome book about frightful flicks, as you strive to ascend to the level of true Horror Freak. From heart-clutching classics like *Dracula* and *Psycho*, and modern masters of mayhem including *Drag Me to Hell*, to lesser known gems such as *Dog Soldiers*, the more 130 movies included in this book are represented in an awesome collection of photos from movie stills and posters.

Item# Z6494 · $19.99